Where some styles of professional mentoring seem to benefit the mentor more than anyone else, Eryl Davies advocates prayer-driven, self-sacrificial, personal investment. He proved this approach for many decades before writing, by being poured out for the sake of the gospel in the lives of countless Christian pastors and workers. The spiritual power of this model can be traced to a simple principle - it calls on mentors to be Christ-like so that their mentees can grow in Christ-likeness.

Ben Fiddian
Pastor, Bonar Bridge and Lairg Free Church, Scotland

This is a helpful introduction and encouragement to form healthy mentoring relationships. The combination of biblical teaching and personal testimonies from a wide variety of contexts, provides a firm foundation from which to flourish.

Jonathan Thomas
Pastor, Cornerstone Church, Abergavenny, Wales;
Author, *Intentional Interruptions: Learning to be Interrupted the Way God Intended*

This is an essential book for those who want to deliberately invest in the spiritual development of other believers. The book comes out of a burden to address the neglected discipline of personal mentoring. Along with clear lessons drawn from the Bible and the author's own experience of church life, we have inspiring testimonies from God's people to provide us with a highly motivational and practical handbook for the Mentor and the Mentee.

Paul Pease
Pastor, Hook Evangelical Church, Surbiton, London

T0016942

Though largely unseen and likely under-utilised, mentoring is a highly valuable ministry. It is warmly explained and commended by Eryl and exemplified by those he gives voice to in this very helpful book.

Jonny Raine
Minister of Pontrhydyrun Baptist Church & Editor of
the Evangelical Magazine

In *The Good Influencer: A Guide to Christian Mentoring*, Eryl Davies takes the myth out of mentoring and makes it understandable and practicable, all the while emphasising the urgent need for it today. This is not just a book about 'how to mentor' but it gives a clear, biblical basis for mentoring drawn from the experiences of Jesus and Paul.

Davies does not limit the book to mere theory or descriptions about mentoring but adds richness and value by sharing the practical experiences of many different people. Utilizing questions to draw out the depth of their mentoring experiences helped to understand what did and did not work.

This book is authentic and is the fruit of a lifetime Dr Davies has spent mentoring others, including myself. I was left challenged to deepen my faith, encouraged to mentor others, and equipped with how to do so well. Highly recommended.

Laura Sanlon
Latin Link and Lausanne Europe

In our day of social media 'influencers' (many inexperienced and undignified), Davies pulls us back to Christian influencing in and for the sake holiness, wisdom, character and experience. Written by a true mentor, Davies practically models what he writes; chiefly as he calls us to listen to others as the Lord Jesus did. This book is an inspirational demonstration of the power of mentoring in the life of the Church.

Natalie Brand
Bible teacher and author of *Priscilla, Where Are You?*
A Call to Joyful Theology

As I read this little book I realised for the first time that, long before I had ever heard the word being used, I had indeed been 'mentored' myself in the early years of my Christian walk and development by an elderly female saint and retired teacher in Stornoway, known locally as 'Miss Christina.' She was a Free Kirk lady of broad ecclesiastical sympathies, and looked out prayerfully for young Christian women, and some young men too, in the local community whom she then took under her wing and sought to instruct more fully in the scriptures and prayer, as well as seeking to broaden our horizons to the vast mission fields of the world. That work was never recognised in any official way by the local church, but I have no doubt that it was fully recognised where it counts, in the heavenly realms. I think too of an elderly lady in my first charge in Barvas, Lewis, who would take the new male converts in the parish under her wing and give them opportunities and encouragement to pray in her home, so preparing them for public prayer in the church. Writing out of his own experience and also out of the experience of many other Christians whose stories are shared in this book, Dr Davies encourages us to consider whether the Lord may be calling us to a mentoring role, whether in our own local community, or in the broader life of the Christian Church today. Is the Lord calling you to such a ministry, even in your old age?'

Hector Morrison
Principal, Highland Theological College, Dingwall

The Good Influencer

A GUIDE TO CHRISTIAN MENTORING

D. Eryl Davies

CHRISTIAN
FOCUS

Copyright © D. Eryl Davies 2023

hardback ISBN 978-1-5271-1003-8
ebook ISBN 978-1-5271-1057-1

Published in 2023 by
Christian Focus Publications Ltd,
Geanies House, Fearn, Ross-shire,
IV20 1TW, Great Britain.
www.christianfocus.com

Cover design by Tom Bernard

Printed and bound by Bell and Bain, Glasgow

Contents

Foreword

This is a much-needed book, offering a masterly treatment of the much neglected practice of mentoring. It is full of pastoral and practical advice undergirded by biblical principles.

I well remember a conversation with a friend who had been in pastoral ministry in Wales for over 40 years. Nearing the end of his public ministry, we were discussing the influence of older men and women on our lives. He commented very warmly and favourably on all the wonderful pastors and preachers who had been models for him in his ministry. He had heard many of them speak at conferences, but I was surprised when he said to me, 'They were such wonderful models as Bible teachers and preachers ... but I just wish one of them had taken time to be with me, to listen to my concerns, and mentor me. I never really had that experience.' As Eryl Davies says in this warm-hearted treatment of the subject of mentoring, the practice has been going on for a long time; however, perhaps in my cultural context, for various reasons, we didn't sufficiently emphasise the practice or encourage one another to exercise this much-needed ministry.

Working with students over the past 40 years, however, I notice that there is much more desire today amongst younger students and student workers to find mentors who can take time to listen to them and invest in them. This book will, therefore, provide a helpful tool for anyone who aspires to be a mentor, or for anyone looking for someone to mentor them. It is so helpful that I plan to purchase 100 copies of this book to pass around the network of 100 evangelists I'm working with in universities around Europe, in the hope that each of them will read the book, seek out mentors for themselves, and offer to mentor younger aspiring evangelists and other Christian workers themselves! Maybe you could do the same?

Dr Davies is judicious when he emphasises that mentoring includes advising, protecting, offering patient, reliable, and kind support. At its heart it demonstrates a concern for the well-being of the whole person. I wish the book had been available when I was in my 20s.

Over my years of involvement in student ministry, I've come across three quotations that encouraged me to invest in the next generation. The first was in a book written by a former leader of the student ministry in India, P. Y. Chandapilla. It was a seminal book entitled *The Master Trainer*, in which he reviewed the ministry of Jesus in the Gospel of Luke, chapters 8 to 10. One Bible verse he mentions in his exposition particularly struck me. It is found in Luke 9:10, after Jesus had called the Twelve to Himself and sent them out with a task, having modelled it himself. The text says that when the apostles returned 'and gave an account to Jesus of all that they had done... Jesus took them with him and withdrew privately to the city of Bethsaida.' It struck me greatly that in the busyness of all His ministry Jesus took time to be alone with His twelve chosen disciples. At the heart of mentoring is the recognition that it is important to deliberately invest quality, unhurried time in individuals or small groups of people. The author points out that Jesus concentrated very much on a few individuals in whom He invested a great deal of time. As we read this book, it may be worth reflecting on our own lives and asking both who invested in us and, the corollary question, 'in whom are we investing?'

Secondly, some years ago when visiting Jamaica, I came across the writings of Keith Panton, a Christian CEO of a bauxite company who wrote a book entitled *Leadership and Citizenship in Post-independence Jamaica,* in which he penned the words, 'The final test of a leader is that he leaves men and women behind him of conviction and with a will to carry on the work he has done. Who are we building up as a contribution to the next generation? We have to keep investing in people.'

As both these books emphasise, investment in individuals is at the heart of mentoring. In this book, Eryl Davies fleshes out practically what this involves in an exceedingly helpful way.

Finally, as I get older, I realise the importance of investing in the next generation. On my desk in my study at home, I have a statement attributed to John Wesley, late in life. I read it each morning:

> For the glory of God,
> Do all the good you can,
> by all the means you can,
> in all the ways you can,
> in all the places you can,
> at all the times you can,
> to all the people you can,
> as long as ever you can.

That, of course, is a broader ministry than the ministry of specifically investing in a few individuals, but it does to some extent capture the vision of focusing not so much on myself and my own ministry, but rather on investing in others. Surely that is at the heart of the ministry of mentoring. The church would therefore be immeasurably strengthened if we took heed of the challenge brought to us by someone who has been involved in mentoring others for decades. I therefore commend this book to you in the hope that it gains wide circulation and leads to a fresh wave of this much-needed, but often much neglected, ministry.

Lindsay Brown
General Secretary, the International Fellowship of
Evangelical Students (IFES), 1991-2007.
International Director, the Lausanne Movement for
World Evangelization, 2008-17.
November 2022

Introduction

After becoming a Christian in College, at the end of his studies Jim obtained employment, then joined a Bible teaching church and almost immediately signed up for the church's discipleship class. The reason? Jim recognised that church commitment and discipling were required of all Christians (Matt. 28:19-20). Months later, a Christian in church asked him whether he would like to be mentored. Jim had no idea what mentoring was so he felt he had no choice but to decline the offer!

Like Jim, the word 'mentoring' was also shrouded in mystery for me. Eventually, I realised I had been mentored by an older Christian, when, in university, one staff worker for UCCF gave me time as we talked and prayed together at regular intervals, spontaneously encouraging me to love and serve the Lord.

Background

Imagine my surprise when some Christian leaders suggested I should write on mentoring.[1] Concerned to encourage Christians with potential for leadership roles in churches and in evangelism, I shared with them the urgent need for mentoring. The following pages are earthed in real pastoral situations, and in a felt need for more mentoring. Others have assisted me by sharing their own experience of mentoring and their stories are fascinating.

---

1. Trustees of the Wales Leadership Forum

Approach

My approach is neither academic nor speculative, but rather grounded in the Bible and illustrated from the experience of contemporary Christians.

You probably have questions you want to ask. Here is one question: Do we need mentoring in a digital age? After all, Google and Alexa are brilliant helps in all kinds of situations. What else do you need? Google is a convenient resource, as is Alexa, a cloud-based voice service. Alexa plays music, makes calls, provides a timer when needed and checks your diary. Then there is all the information available concerning the weather, traffic, sport, tasks to do, and a host of other things. Alexa and Google are always there for you. Who needs a mentor? Well, neither Google nor Alexa can provide a close real-life relationship or supply us with the wisdom and encouragement we need. Family and work tensions, suffering, disappointments, difficult choices, bereavement, personal development, spiritual growth and Christian work or ministry are not areas where either Google or Alexa excel. Often there are no obvious answers to some challenges in life. An experienced person who listens and wisely encourages, then advises from Scripture and experience, is far superior to platforms like Google or Alexa.

In the next two chapters, we will answer basic questions about mentoring, so please read on and accompany me and my friends on this exciting journey! Yes, the book is about mentoring. More importantly, it is about people and, strategically, it is about future leaders in churches and in evangelism. Even more importantly, it is all about honouring the Lord Jesus Christ in our lives and witness. And that is more important than anything else.

Chapter 1

What is Mentoring?

What follows in the next two chapters is a sample of key questions you may be asking about mentoring. The answers are brief as some will be explained further in later chapters.

Q 1: Is mentoring something new?

A: No. The concept is often traced back to Homer's *Odyssey*, an ancient Greek epic poem in which Odysseus committed his young son, Telemachus, to the care of a person named Mentor, while he himself went to fight in the Trojan war. For Mentor, caring for the boy involved advising, protecting, and ensuring his happiness and education. Later, Socrates mentored the famous Greek philosopher Plato, who, in turn, mentored Aristotle. Mentoring is not a new idea.

Q 2: Why is mentoring a buzzword today?

A: One reason is that the business world discovered its value years ago and uses it extensively. For example, the giant motor company *Ford* has its own mentoring programme for the purpose of improving company culture, and linking what is often a diverse and remote workforce. Their aim is to increase productivity and secure staff retention by using mentoring. For *Intel*, its mentoring programme is focused on peer-to-peer mentoring, with employees encouraged to pursue their own mentorships. In small businesses, mentoring is deemed useful in providing advice, direction, stability, and well-being for staff as well as encouraging personal development. Interestingly, Michelle Obama (nee Robinson) was designated as Barack's mentor at the law firm where they both worked while he was a summer associate. Barack frequently credits her as being the support and success behind his considerable achievements. To meet this growing demand for mentoring, there are various courses geared to equipping individuals for their careers.

Q 3: Can you give examples of mentoring in the business/ entertainment world?

A: One example is the founder of Facebook, Mark Zuckerberg, who needed advice and mentoring in a tough patch during the early period of Facebook. He respected the Apple entrepreneur, Steve Jobs, so they met, and Jobs provided him with invaluable encouragement and guidance over a period. When Jobs died in 2011, Zuckerberg posted: 'Steve, thank you for being a mentor and friend. Thanks for showing that what you build can change the world. I will miss you.'[1] Richard Branson used Sir Freddie Laker to enable him to get his Virgin Atlantic Airways company off the ground. Branson claimed: 'If you ask any successful business person, they will always have had a great mentor at some point along the road.' He then admitted: 'I wouldn't have got anywhere in the airline industry without the mentorship of Sir Freddie Laker', the once Surrey and England cricketer. [2]

Celebrities have valued mentoring. The American TV celebrity, Oprah Winfrey was mentored for years by the poet Maya Angelou. Their friendship began when Oprah was in her twenties, embarking on her career as a reporter. Maya's influence and advice made a huge difference to Oprah's life

---

1. People & Celebrities, October 6, 2011, Lucas Shaw.
2. Airliner World, 8 August, 2022

and career, leading Oprah to describe Maya as her 'mentor-mother-sister-friend'.

In the film industry, one outstanding example of mentoring was Audrey Hepburn, who mentored Elizabeth Taylor, among others. Taylor was mentored by Hepburn throughout her career and they remained close friends until the latter's death in 1993. Similarly, mentoring is used in sport, but more frequently it is identified with, and restricted to, coaching and training. On the other hand, mentoring is often undertaken intentionally or spontaneously by individuals who feel the need for a trusted and experienced person to advise and encourage them, often over a significant period of time. This can happen within a family or among friends or within a Christian church.

Q 4: What is mentoring?

A: A mentor often gives advice, but encouraging, listening, sharing, supporting, guiding, and motivating are essential features of mentoring. Another major feature is that of influence, which can be profound even though there may be no formal mentoring. Influencing may be a better word to use than mentoring, but remember that mentoring is different from coaching, counselling, training, or therapy. The mentor needs to be accessible, trustworthy, caring, competent, and reasonably experienced, as well as respected in terms of character, wisdom, experience, and compatibility.

Q 5: What are the main aspects of Christian mentoring?

A: Normally two main aspects of mentoring in general are recognised. One aspect is *career related*, particularly the mentee's progress and development in work-related situations, including involvement in a church or a Christian organisation. The mentee needs advice, acceptance, counsel, training, and encouragement, so the mentor has experience and wisdom to share. The second aspect is providing *personal*

17

support by encouraging, advising, and praying with, and for, the mentee, as well as being a role model.

Q 6: Is this true of all mentoring?

A: There are differences. For example, in business mentoring there can be a stronger focus on career-related aspects, such as developing skills and adapting the mentee to the culture of the workplace, but less time given to more personal aspects. On the other hand, the business and commercial world recognise the importance of encouraging the mentee, and providing personal support as well as professional guidance. In Christian mentoring, the mentor is respected for their knowledge, but especially for their lifestyle, experience, and trustworthiness. They will be patient, supportive, reliable, kind, committed, available and, most importantly, Christ-like, so they become an influential role model.

Q 7: Is mentoring the same as coaching?

A: Coaching and mentoring are very different. A coach instructs a person or a team on how to achieve success in areas like education or sport, so skills are developed personally and as a team; the focus is on *how* to improve and succeed. The coach is experienced but also friendly, rather than impatient or controlling. Too often, a coach can be guilty of physical and psychological abuse, which highlights the need for holiness on the part of any Christian involved in coaching and mentoring. The latter is more relational than coaching, with its concern for the whole person in guiding and encouraging the mentee in their lives and work, whether they are successful or not.

Q 8: What does the Bible say about mentoring?

A: As you may expect, the Bible says a great deal about mentoring; however, I give you two helpful examples as a starter. In 1 Thessalonians 2:7-12, Paul's preaching had led to the formation and growth of a local church in Thessalonica, and within a brief period of time. Paul, the preacher, also pastored and mentored the young Christians by living a consistent life, and caring like a nurse/mother and a father for their children. This mentoring aspect included guiding, encouraging and instructing believers practically; see verses 7-12. Another example is found in Titus 2:3-5, where older women with good character in the church are expected to mentor and guide younger women, especially in their family situation, showing them how to love their husbands and children but also generally to live as an example in all aspects of their lives.

Q 9: How does Christian mentoring differ from 'pastoring'?

A: In addition to a church 'pastor', all Christians 'pastor' by caring spiritually and practically for each other in a church or group. The needs and circumstances of individuals being pastored vary, but pastoring involves caring and being alongside them in encouraging them to trust, honour, and know God in their specific needs. All Christians need to care for others prayerfully in church.

Mentoring includes this element of pastoring, but rather than having a specific spiritual or practical problem, a mentee is supported in serving the Lord by having someone with Christian experience and knowledge available to pray with and discuss situations, or use their personal gifts in order to encourage or advise. Frequently, a mentee is being equipped and supported in their Christian work. Pastoring involves this mentoring role, so no sharp distinction must be drawn between the two. Ideally, there is a long-term relationship of trust and sharing where the mentee develops confidence in living for Christ in church, in society, and in the family unit, supported by a mentor.

Q 10: How does mentoring differ from discipling?

A: An overlap exists because discipling and mentoring often merge into one another, but there are differences. The word 'discipling' appears in the Lord's commission to the Church in Matthew 28:19-20, and is translated as 'make disciples'. This is a command rather than an option, so all the church is involved in this task in various ways.

Discipling involves:
a. Sharing the gospel with unbelievers until an individual trusts in the Lord Jesus Christ; then the discipling process begins in instructing converts in God's Word and the major doctrines of the Christian faith.
b. Discipling continues in encouraging converts to live a Christ-pleasing life in their families, church, and society.
c. Discipling can continue for weeks or months until a Christian is established in their faith and settled in a Bible-teaching church.

Mentoring, by contrast, assumes that the Christian is discipled, integrated into a church, and following the Lord. Often, a Christian being mentored is involved in Christian work voluntarily, or in a part- or full-time capacity, and therefore benefits from having a mentor to liaise with and share personal, as well as work pressures and concerns confidentially. Wise encouragement is needed for individuals with leadership potential in facing new situations or challenges, so a strong relational context is encouraged in which experience is shared prayerfully and biblically.

Q 11: Who is qualified to be a mentor?

A: In a Christian context, a mentor must be a Christian, but some lack the aptitude or temperament to mentor another Christian, while others lack wisdom, Bible knowledge, or experience of serving the Lord. A mentor also needs to be prayerful, respected as a reasonably mature Christian, faithful to Christ, with a love for people. Other qualities needed include trustworthiness, reliability, confidentiality, objectivity, and especially that they are living lives pleasing to the Lord. Mentors should model Christian character and need to be able to encourage quality service for the Lord, but definitely must not be boring, heavy, negative, or critical. Christians who mentor often acknowledge their own weaknesses, but compassion, wisdom, trust, prayerfulness, and a deep interest in, and regard for, the mentee are qualities that are most attractive and fruitful.

Q 12: How do you find or recognise a potential mentee?

A: That is a difficult question to answer. As I have prayed for an individual and heard of their commitment to Christ and desire to serve the Lord, I have felt drawn to that person. Following opportunities to talk to the individual and to develop a relationship, this can lead to a spontaneous sharing at a deeper level in which mentoring occurs. This is not imposed, but mentor and mentee are drawn into a warm relationship of trust, love, and prayer without any pressure.

A potential mentee may be suggested by someone in the church or Christian Union, but there is no one way of finding a mentee. Christians who feel the need of being mentored should develop good relationships within their local church or Christian Union, and get to know other believers well. This may lead to a closer relationship with someone and a mentoring relationship may develop naturally. One is looking in a mentee for a heart to love and live for the Lord, as well as an openness to be mentored.

In the next chapter we will ask further questions about mentoring.

Chapter 2

Finding a Mentor

There are more questions requiring our attention and they concern finding a mentor, possible abuse in mentoring, and also different ways of mentoring.

Q 13: 'How can I find a Christian to mentor me?'

A. I emphasise again that some are not gifted to be mentors. Others feel unworthy, even inferior, and fearful to mentor and need mentoring themselves. Some claim they are too busy or feel threatened by a possible mentoring relationship and uncertain of the demands which may be made on them. However, there is a lack of teaching concerning mentoring and caring for one another, and too often ongoing pastoral care is deficient. Young Christians, even after following a discipleship course, can be left to themselves to benefit from church meetings without further thought to their spiritual development and potential for leadership. Superficial levels of fellowship amongst Christians are not always conducive to spiritual development. Don't despair! Your great need is to love and trust Christ, then model Him in your life. You may then, in the Lord's providence, be drawn into a mentoring relationship, even if that term is not employed. If there is a Christian you respect and think you can learn from, why not ask if you could meet regularly in person or online? Another option is to ask one of the church leaders or Christian Union leaders if they can help in linking Christians together for mentoring and accountability.

Q 14: Why do more women not mentor younger women?

A: Perhaps more mentoring is being undertaken by women than is recognised and they are doing it more naturally, while some are excellent and mentor quietly and spontaneously without calling it mentoring. Are women encouraged to mentor, especially older women mentoring younger women (Titus 2:1-5)? Women often feel more free to request help or offer to help and mentor others. Amongst younger women, there is evidence in some Christian Unions and church youth groups that they are mentoring their peers or those younger than themselves. This is spontaneous, but more teaching and encouragement are required, which also applies to men mentoring men, especially younger men.

Q 15: Is it appropriate for a man to mentor a woman?

A: There is a nervousness on the part of some men over mentoring a woman. The sexual misconduct and misuse of power on the part of people in society (which has sadly, at times, included Christians), is disturbing. In mentoring, confidentiality and depth of sharing can lead, if not extremely careful, to a misuse of the situation, or even wrong expectations from a mentee or mentor, so there can be a climate of fear – and rightly so. Provided necessary safeguards are in place, alongside mutual respect and godly living, then it is appropriate in some situations for a male to mentor a female, but if a suitable woman is available to serve as mentor then that may be more appropriate. However, directive against a male-female mentoring relationship could have negative implications for women in being deprived of invaluable wisdom, experience, support and prayer from a male mentor. One hears of women leaders claiming that an important key to their development has been quality mentoring by a man.

Q 16: Are there warning signs concerning mentoring?

A: There are three major warning signs to be highlighted:

Abuse

One warning sign is that of *abuse,* which is expressed in varying forms whether physical, psychological, emotional, spiritual, or financial abuse. Bullying and control is one example where a mentor can expect to be obeyed and their advice accepted without question. When this happens, it is wise to end the relationship, whoever the person may be, even a pastor, elder, or the leader of a Christian organisation. Bullying and mind-control sadly exist amongst Christians. Beware!

Or as the relationship develops, physical abuse may rear its ugly head, and inappropriate language, gestures, and advances used to take advantage of a mentee. In our contemporary society, where domestic abuse and other forms of physical and sexual abuse are rife, this must not be tolerated in any relationship. If this is happening to you, you should seek help immediately.

Intrusion

A second warning sign is when a mentor is *intrusive* by prying into the private life of the mentee unnecessarily. This can occur without the mentee recognising it at first because there is a thin line between sharing personal matters for encouragement, guidance, and prayer, and someone exploiting this for his or her own satisfaction. A mentor has a responsibility not to divulge confidential information about the individual, but also not to pursue unnecessary information that should remain private. It can be easy for a mentor to take advantage of a mentee, so privacy must be respected at all times and boundaries set.

Dependency

This third warning is necessary. The mentee must *not be made to feel dependent* on that relationship, so that without it their lives would disintegrate. There is a degree of dependence on a counsellor or mentor that in some situations is necessary for a relatively brief period, but the aim must always be to enable the person to go forward confidently to live for the Lord without depending on another person. Wisdom is required in such relationships with the object of pointing individuals consistently to the Lord and His Word, rather than encouraging dependence on a mentor or a pastor.

Q 17: *Are there different ways for Christians to use mentoring?*

A: Yes. A helpful form of mentoring is the one-to-one relationship based on face-to-face or virtual meetings, supplemented by social media or phone calls to maintain contact. One can also mentor a small group where there is a shared focus, but there needs to be mutual trust, integrity, and confidentiality. There can also be peer-to-peer mentoring where someone of a similar age, but with more experience or knowledge, mentors. This often happens in church youth groups or school/college Christian Unions when a Christian, possibly only a year or two older, or even the same age but with more Christian maturity, can mentor a peer in valuable and spontaneous ways. There is also inter-generational mentoring when older people mentor someone younger. There is a wealth of experience and wisdom older people can share. Flexibility, therefore, is required.

We take a closer look at this in the next chapter.

Chapter 3

What Mentoring Looks Like in Practice

Allow me to share two relationships that were formative in my earlier years, but in different ways. Both were important.

The first was in my mid-teens where, for a period of five years, our local church elder showed considerable interest in what I was doing, particularly in my early career, then my entry into training for the Christian ministry. Tom Gordon had the top job with the Post Office in Merseyside. He was not theologically discerning, but he worked hard in the church and cared about the young people. Was he a mentor? Not really, although he was an extremely generous and affable person. He and his wife always encouraged me and others; they were hospitable. They wanted me to succeed whether in sport, industry, or college. Later I shared with him my 'call' to the Christian ministry. He was supportive, immediately starting the process for testing my call and eventual acceptance for training within the denomination. He was an adviser and encourager, but not a mentor. At the time, however, I needed his support and encouragement.

Consider a different relationship. While in university, the new staff member of the UCCF[1] in Wales unexpectedly called to see me. I had heard him speak but this was the first opportunity for us to talk together. I was a young Christian, but he had been a pastor and had experienced God working

---

1. Universities and Colleges Christian Fellowship

powerfully. He shared his burden for the Lord's work in Wales, and wanted to encourage me. He was attentive, probing, and prayed with me. We met regularly afterwards, praying together and discussing the Lord's work. He was the Rev. J. Elwyn Davies.[2]

Prayer

One experience stands out for me. Near the end of one academic term, Elwyn Davies suggested at short notice that I should go home with him that night to Bala in North Wales, spend the night with his family, then the following day spend some hours with him in prayer for the Lord's work in the University. Providentially, it was an unforgettable experience. Without realising, I was being mentored, encouraged, and introduced to the dimension of prayer. I felt as if I had been paddling in the sea as a young Christian, but he led me into a deeper experience of the Lord. The word, mentoring, was never used; his burden was to encourage, advise, pray with, train, and support Christians like myself for leadership positions in churches. It was visionary on his part, and influential. His influence was profound.

When I became a church pastor, this man continued to mentor me, but in less obvious ways. He showed interest in what I was doing and contacted me at regular intervals. Sometimes we met in conferences or committees and he often took the initiative in spending time with me over a coffee. I knew he cared and was available for me—and for many others too. When I occasionally asked him questions, he was prepared to give time to discuss them; even when he himself was extremely busy, he made time to share and pray with me. On one occasion when I found public prayer difficult, his answer left a deep impression upon me. He

2. See my "Introduction" in *A Father In The Faith: J. Elwyn Davies, 1925-2007*, Edited by John Emyr (Bridgend: Bryntirion Press, 2012), 13-41; "Rhagymadrodd", *Porth Yr Aur: Cofio J. Elwyn Davies*, golygwyd gan John Emyr (Pen-y-bont ar Ogwr, Wasg Bryntirion, 2011), 11-43.

advised me there was no quick-fix concerning praying in public, either in leading a service or praying in a prayer meeting. His answer was the same – one's own personal prayer life and relationship with the Lord were the key areas I needed to focus on if I was to engage more freely in public prayer. Then I valued his wisdom, graciousness, and the way he placed prayer at the centre of his own life and ministry. That meant that when we were together, however briefly or long, praying was given a significant place in our time together.

I thank God for the way he cared for, advised, prayed for, and supported me, sometimes in difficult situations. Mentors like him can have an enormous influence in our lives.

Chapter 4

Help! Where Are the Mentors?

That is a heart cry from some young and older Christians who want to be mentored by a Christian they respect. They want to live for the Lord and serve Him better. The cry goes up – where are the mentors? But why is mentoring rare? Here are a few thoughts relating to the lack of mentoring:

One reason we have referred to is that many do not know what mentoring is, so there is need for teaching.

A **second** reason relates to a failure to recognise the need for mentoring, possibly related to assumptions made by Christian leaders. For example, it is suggested that the main means of grace such as Sunday preaching meetings and weeknight Bible study/prayer meetings are adequate for Christians, especially when supplemented in Christian fellowship. There is no need for mentoring.

Mentoring is never intended as a substitute for the means of grace when the church meets to hear God's Word and pray together. Mentoring is supplementary, more personal, and seeks to encourage and develop the potential and gifts of an individual in going on with the Lord and serving Him. Some may soon become church leaders or assume leadership in a Christian movement aiming to evangelise and disciple people. Here is an additional need not necessarily met by the means of grace.

A **third** reason is that some Christian leaders have no time to mentor. Some Christian leaders are under enormous pressure and even suffer discouragement, burnout, and exhaustion. One must feel sympathy, for, too often, pastors or other leaders do not receive the support or understanding required.

A **fourth** reason is that a leader can doubt whether he or she is suitable for, or even capable of, being a mentor. The subject of mentoring may arouse a sense of fear and inadequacy, which often may not be expressed but is felt keenly by those who struggle in some areas of their lives and their work for the Lord. They need to be understood and mentored too!

A **fifth** reason is that often Christian leaders are unaware of the needs of others, which can be due to a lack of good interpersonal relationships and skills. What do I mean? There are several aspects that need teasing out here. For example, fellowship between Christians is often at a superficial level and conversations after and between meetings, even if reasonably serious, remain at a relatively superficial level, without developing into more personal engagement with individuals. Christian fellowship, of course, is much more than sharing a coffee or cake after a meeting, talking about the weather, health, work, or family. How can we get beyond polite, general conversation and fellowship to share real needs? Acceptance of one another, mutual respect, confidentiality, and genuine love are required to move forward in this area, with the need for one or two individuals to take the initiative in breaking through these 'polite' barriers in fellowship sensitively, without being brash and overbearing.

There is need, especially for leaders, to know their people well pastorally, and to care. We are all different in terms of personality, temperament, and background, but often shyness can keep us back from sharing openly, or even approaching someone who needs support. One lesson I learned was the value of listening to what people say. Too often in conversation a person may not really be listening and may then be perceived as being disinterested. Genuinely listening to people is an indication to a person that we care, and care enough to listen well. Here is one way we can engage in genuine fellowship and begin to know one another better.

There is one **final** reason why mentors in Christian circles may be in short supply. Too many Christians are ill-equipped to serve as a mentor. Let me explain. I meet young Christians in their teens and twenties who are serious in living out the principles of Matthew 6:33: *'But seek first the kingdom of God and His righteousness; and all these things shall be added to you.'* They are passionate about loving and honouring Christ in their lives. They are eager to serve the Lord well. Some have considerable leadership potential and need to be encouraged, advised, prayed for, and befriended. A mentor needs at least to be as Christ-like as *they* are and be respected for his/her lifestyle and commitment to Christ.

I re-emphasise the need for more quality mentors, especially for young Christians. Age is not the determining factor but rather integrity, Christ-likeness, and a deep interest and concern to see believers growing in grace and being enabled to live their Christian lives consistently and fruitfully. Prayer needs to be at the heart of any mentoring relationship, as well as trust and confidentiality. Could you, with the Lord's enabling and grace, become a mentor for a young Christian, irrespective of age difference?

Mentoring has been described as 'the missing key' in equipping Christians. Underlying this question is disappointment regarding the lifestyle and lack of spirituality of Christians, including peers. This is a generalization, of course, yet young Christians need an example of consistent Christian living that they can respect and follow. And they are not alone. Kevin DeYoung, in his book *The Hole in our Holiness*, thinks there 'is something missing in the contemporary church scene', namely consistent Christ-centred living, marked by obedience and a passionate love for the Lord.[1]

There is more. A reasonable grasp of the Bible is needed, and wisdom in relating God's Word to situations and varying needs. Maturity in the Christian life and a prayerfulness that is authentic in private life, as well as in meetings, are qualities that are essential in mentoring. To be able to share concerning our ongoing personal experience of the Lord and what we are learning about Him in the Word are, again, important for a mentor. You may think you are not qualified to mentor. That's how I always feel, but by the Lord's grace and the Holy Spirit's enabling we are privileged to model the Christian life. Where are the mentors? They are amongst us, but we need to practise Matthew 6:33 and take our privileges and responsibilities seriously. Are we living under the lordship of Christ?

---

1. Kevin DeYoung, *The Hole in our Holiness* (Wheaton: Crossway, 2012), 12.

Chapter 5

Model Mentoring: The Lord Jesus Christ

The Bible is God's book; it is unique, accurate, and authoritative. The Holy Spirit ensured that those writing the Bible at different times wrote accurately (2 Pet. 1:21; 2 Tim. 3:16-17) what God unveiled concerning His character and purpose. The Bible, therefore, is incredibly rich in its content and breadth. That is why we turn to the Bible for teaching, guidance, and comfort.

Background

1. The Old Testament has two commonly used Hebrew words relating to leadership and translated as 'guiding', 'leading', or 'directing'. One word is in Psalm 48:14: 'He will be our guide even to death.' The covenantal, compassionate God is 'our guide' and King, leading us securely and wisely 'to the end'. In Isaiah 49:10, the same word is used in describing God's compassionate care, love, and provision for His people, even in unlikely places, as God directed them to the Promised Land. Interestingly, the second of four Servant Songs in Isaiah, pointing to Christ, appears in this chapter from verses 1-7 but may include verses 8-12. Christ is the ultimate, unique Servant portrayed in all four songs in Isaiah.

2. Christians who lead at varying levels are expected to express the Lord's love and care towards all who are in

Christ. According to 1 Samuel 13:14, the Lord seeks leaders 'after His own heart', and this includes all who train, mentor, care for and pastor others.

3. Different words are used in the New Testament to describe leadership/mentoring. In 1 Thessalonians 5:12 a leader is 'over' believers in leading, protecting, and caring, and so should be respected and imitated in terms of their faith and behaviour (Heb. 13:7, 17). Both the Gospels and the Epistles emphasise calling, character, humility, and service rather than power or position (Luke 22:25-26). 1 Peter 5:2-3 confirms this pattern for any leader in the Lord's work by using the shepherd image, which is deeply embedded in the Old Testament. Peter here uses a play on words which can be translated as 'shepherd the sheep', with Peter using the same word the Lord Jesus used when telling him: 'tend my sheep' (John 21:15-17). The shepherd imagery is used powerfully by the Lord in John 10:1-21 where He, above all others, is the 'good shepherd'.

I am focusing briefly on two examples of mentoring in the New Testament. The first is our Lord's perfect example of training/mentoring His disciples, and the second is the apostle Paul's mentoring of Christian leaders. While there are other examples in the Bible, these two provide us with superb teaching concerning mentoring.

The Lord Jesus Christ

Our Lord's mentoring of His apostles serves as the greatest model of all.

Context

1. After praying all night to His Father (Luke 6:12), the Lord Jesus chose twelve apostles, a term from a verb meaning *'to send'*. Their main task would be preaching (Mark 3:13-19). 'The Twelve' were very different in background, occupation, personality, and gifts, but for three years they accompanied

the Lord Jesus almost everywhere. They listened to His teaching, witnessed His miracles, observed His flawless life of love and obedience, witnessing also how He prayed, then cared for people. Theirs was a huge privilege, but a learning curve, to be with the Son of God incarnate. The Lord was preparing them for their unique leadership in churches after He returned to heaven (Acts 1:4-11), with Peter and John having key roles in the growth and oversight of churches beyond Pentecost (Acts 2).

2. The apostles had no successors because their role was foundational in leading/overseeing the church from Pentecost onwards until their deaths. Nevertheless, there are principles and aspects of that training that have permanent value, so we identify key aspects of mentoring as exemplified in His training of the apostles.

How did the Lord Jesus mentor?

I am using the word 'mentoring' as an acronym, spelling out aspects of mentoring. Here is an outline:

M = Modelling a life that glorifies God
E = Encouragment
N = Need
T = Teaching
O = Openness
R = Relational
I = Intentional
N = Nurturing
G = Gentleness.

M = *Modelling a life which glorifies God.*

The Lord Jesus practised in His life and ministry what He preached. Those who lived with Him and watched Him closely in public and private could say He 'committed no sin, nor was deceit found in His mouth' (1 Pet. 2:22; Isa. 53:9). In instructing His disciples to 'seek first the kingdom of God and His righteousness…' (Matt. 6:33), that is what He did throughout His life. 'I do not seek My own will,' He explained, 'but the will of the Father who sent Me' (John 5:30, 6:38; Luke 22:42). No one could accuse Him of hypocrisy or living a double life (Heb. 7:26). The Bible describes the entire life and death of Jesus Christ as one of complete obedience culminating in Him becoming 'obedient to the point of death, even the death of the cross' (Phil. 2:8). The physical, emotional, and spiritual sufferings He endured on the cross were infinite, but a necessary part of His obedience in bearing the punishment for our sins. That obedience was never cold or clinical but expressed in love, compassion, and care for people, whatever their needs. Love and compassion cascaded from Him like a mighty river, often in contrast to the hardness and selfishness of the disciples (Matt. 14:15-18; Mark 9:38-41; Luke 18:15-17) and religious leaders.

Anyone involved in training, teaching, and mentoring must endeavour to model Christ in their lives as 'obedient children' (1 Pet. 1:14; John 14:15) and grow more like Christ daily.

E = *Encouragement*

Advising, supporting, modelling, guiding, sharing wisdom, and praying, at times even laughing and relaxing, are essential features of mentoring but so is encouragement. For example, the Sermon on the Mount in Matthew's Gospel (chapters 5-7) is packed with solid teaching, but the Lord also urged His disciples not to worry, encouraging them to trust their heavenly Father who feeds the birds and clothes the grass and flowers. God the Father will also feed and clothe His followers (Matt. 6:25-34). Again, in chapters 14-16 of John's Gospel, in their perplexity and sorrow because their Lord was leaving them, they are encouraged as Jesus explains carefully why He was going to the Father. There is an abundance of comfort and encouragement in these chapters, before the Lord went on to pray for them and all believers in chapter seventeen. In a post-resurrection appearance to His disciples, He questioned Peter three times concerning his love for Him (John 21:15-19). Despite his denial, Peter was not abandoned or removed from his key role of preaching and leadership. Too often a mentor or church leader can discourage and be angry with a mentee unnecessarily when the need is for gentle encouragement. The latter is often in short supply!

N = *Need*

Both the mentor and mentee have needs in what should be a reciprocal and collaborative relationship. Open, supportive fellowship with a mentee often benefits the mentor in surprising ways. I can anticipate your question! Did the Lord Jesus have needs as He mentored the disciples? He was neither troubled by indwelling sin, as we are, nor was He guilty of unbelief. However, physical tiredness and hunger were very real to Him (Mark 4:38), as well as sorrow. He 'wept' before raising Lazarus from the dead (John 11:35) then, in anticipating His death on the cross, He exclaimed: 'Now My soul is troubled', or agitated (John 12:27). In comforting His sad disciples (John 14:1), little did they realise how deeply perturbed and distressed He was in His thoughts and emotions in anticipating the cross. In the garden of Gethsemane, He knew loneliness and what it was to be forsaken by friends and even by His Father on the cross as He suffered for our sins (Matt. 26:40; 27:46). While mentors have needs, the needs of the mentee ought to be uppermost in the mentor's mind in encouraging, supporting, advising, and developing them in their walk with the Lord and their engagement in Christian work.

T = *Teaching*

Central to our Lord's training and mentoring of the apostles was the element of teaching; thus, in a mentoring relationship, sharing and applying God's Word in the context of personal need and development is foundational. In Matthew's Gospel there are five major blocks of teaching consisting of discourses given on different occasions (chapters 5-7; 10; 13; 18; 23-25), while in John's Gospel we find the prologue (1:1-18), the Lord's self-disclosure in word and deed (1:19-10:42), the Life and death of the King and Suffering Servant (11:1-12:50), then His further self-disclosure in His cross and exaltation (13:1-20:31) followed by the epilogue (21:1-25). John's Gospel represents 'an interlocking' tradition where all four Gospels 'mutually reinforce or explain each other' in recording the Lord's teaching and ministry.[1] You can do no better than read and re-read carefully all four Gospels and study how the Lord Jesus taught. Here I make four observations relevant to mentoring:

1) Mentoring involves more than teaching the Word. Teaching should be available in a local church and also in appropriate specialised courses, while there are discipleship classes for young converts where basic teaching is provided in a church to nurture Christians in the faith. Teaching is not the whole story.

2) Frequently, the Lord asked His disciples whether they understood what He was teaching (for example, Matt. 15:16; Mark 4:13). Friendly, non-threatening, and informal questioning is a useful aspect of mentoring in unpacking and applying doctrine and biblical principles to specific situations, and in this way, securing development and spiritual maturity. For example, there may be a failure to grasp and relate the objective and definitive nature of justification or sanctification, especially if a mentee is

---

1. D. A. Carson, *The Gospel According to John*, (Leicester/Grand Rapids: IVP, 1991), 52.

troubled by discouragement, introspection, or a loss of self-esteem. Sometimes, help is needed in facing criticism in Christian work and relationships, or advice is required in communicating a gospel message.

3) It is important in mentoring not to overload hearers with teaching or demands. The Lord's wisdom is expressed in John 16:12: 'I still have many things to say to you, but you cannot bear them now.' Patiently and gradually applying the Word encourages, rather than overwhelms, a mentee or even a congregation, so wisdom is required on the part of the mentor.

4) Maintaining the big picture of God's redemptive purpose is also necessary. Personal circumstances may be difficult, so the mentee may feel discouraged. Therefore, reflecting on the glorious redemptive purpose of God can develop more biblical and objective thinking concerning their circumstances. This can be heart warming, especially for a person struggling with circumstances, a sense of failure, and weakness. Or, a mentee may be unwise in preaching the doctrine of God's wrath to those with no concept of the holy character of God. That can be disastrous. The Lord Jesus, for example, used the teaching of hell sensitively, depending on the condition and attitude of His audience. He did not preach hell indiscriminately. He knew His audiences well and used that doctrine only after people had been under His teaching, and when there was hardening and mounting opposition. This is especially true in Luke 16:19-31 where He warns and gives the most detailed account of the after-life that He ever gave in the Gospels.[2] Normally, the big picture of the redemptive purpose of the triune God and our place in that purpose is what dominated His teaching and mentoring.

---

2. Eryl Davies, *Preaching – An Awesome Task: Wrath, Final Judgement, Hell and the Glorious Gospel*, (Bridgend: Bryntirion Press, 2016), 87-94.

O = *Openness*

In reading the four Gospels, one is impressed by the openness of the Lord Jesus to the needs of people around Him and the unexpected demands made on Him. He was open in responding to the pressing needs and suffering of people, despite the attitude of His disciples on occasions (Mark 5:31, 6:35-39; Luke 9:37-42, 18:15-17). His openness flowed from deep compassion, so people were attracted to Him. The same openness was evident in relation to the disciples during the three years they spent together. Openness to the needs and circumstances of others is required in all who mentor, but coupled with a willingness for our timetable to be re-scheduled unexpectedly in responding to an urgent call from a mentee for help. Underlying such openness is a trust and warmth, which makes a mentor approachable and accessible at any time.

R = *Relational*

Mentoring is deeply relational, demanding close bonds of trust, respect, and love with a mentee. A mentoring relationship develops slowly at first and its length is variable, but often the mentoring can continue for years. For the twelve apostles, the mentoring spanned a period of three years, but they lived with their mentor, and accompanied Him almost everywhere, observing and listening to Him daily during that period. This mentoring was strongly relational, as the Lord spent time with them, teaching, encouraging, and mentoring them. His approach, therefore, was highly relational in showing a deep interest in them personally, and as a group. To express the point differently, mentoring, for the Lord, was not an occasional, haphazard, or dutiful conversation with a mentee who is then forgotten until the next scheduled meeting. Far from it. In this relationship, there are expectations, with a mentee often longing to develop as a Christian and in his or her work for the

Lord. There are matters to share, discuss, and pray over, so meetings may need to be more regular. As the relationship is being forged, prayer for one another, mutual concern, and love, with an eagerness to see the mentee becoming more useful to the Lord, are integral elements in that relationship.

Quite often the Lord used informal occasions away from the crowds, where He talked informally with the disciples. The element of informality within an agreed structure appeals as being natural and effective. The Lord visited the home of Peter's mother-in-law, whom He healed of a dangerous fever, and afterwards enjoyed a meal there (Mark 1:29-31). After speaking to the crowds, He entered another house where the apostles were able to question Him informally (Matt. 13:36). After walking with His disciples through Galilee, He entered a house with them where He asks what they had been discussing while walking (Mark 9:33). He frequently shared a meal with His disciples (Mark 14:12-21) or occasionally breakfast by the seaside (John 21:1-15). The apostles bonded with their Lord partly by means of His care, approachability, and even His informality. A coffee or a meal is often conducive to our sharing, but developing a relationship of trust is extremely important.

I = *Intentional*

The Lord chose the twelve apostles with the intention of training and mentoring them, intending to make them 'fishers of men' (Matt. 4:19), so teaching and mentoring them were not delegated to others during the three-year period as He exposed them to different situations, challenges, and responsibilities. How can we express this intentionality regarding mentoring today?

The *first step* is that Churches, mission agencies, and Christian Unions must understand what mentoring is and what it involves. That is the first and essential step.

The *next step* is to identify intentionally those individuals with leadership potential and a passion for Christ, so prayer and wisdom are needed.

A *third step* is to identify and encourage suitable mentors, with the vision of them having a key role in equipping and supporting mentees.

Fourthly, in this process of identifying suitable mentors and mentees, quality pastoral care is a key component, which involves knowing individuals well in different age groups.

N = *Nurturing*

The Oxford Dictionary defines nurturing as 'a process of bringing up or training', 'fostering care', exercising an 'influence' or providing 'nourishment'. Mentoring is a process that can be lengthy or relatively brief, if circumstances dictate, but nurturing is gradual, as mentor and mentee talk and pray together. Patience and commitment are required and normally a mentor and the mentee must be committed to a process over a period of time, sometimes for years! Mentoring involves fostering care in guiding and supporting the mentee forward in living for the Lord and serving Him. No one should enter a mentor-mentee relationship without intending to commit seriously to this process of nurturing and development.

G = *Gentleness*

Dane Ortland's book *Gentle and Lowly* has the sub-title *The Heart of Christ for Sinners and Sufferers.*[3] This is a valuable book explaining that the Lord Jesus Christ, the Son of God, is *'gentle and lowly'* (Matt. 11:29). Ortland writes: 'What is most true of him is that he is "gentle and lowly." These two words mean He is humble and meek. Ortland notes that 'Jesus is not trigger-happy. Not harsh, reacting, easily

---

3.   Dane Ortland, *Gentle and Lowly: The Heart of Christ for Sinners and Sufferers* (Wheaton: Crossway, 2020), 19-21.

exasperated. He is the most understanding person in the universe. The posture most natural to him is not a pointed finger but open arms.[4] He is 'accessible … no one in human history has ever been more approachable than Jesus Christ… No hoops to jump through'. Gentle and lowly in heart, 'this is who he is. Tender. Open. Welcoming. Accommodating. Understanding. Willing.' If you are mentoring or considering mentoring, you need to be like the Lord Jesus in terms of love, gentleness, accessibility, and humility. If you want a mentor, this is the kind of person you need. You have been warned!

In the next chapter we look at the way in which the apostle Paul mentored.

---

4.   Dane Ortland, *Gentle and Lowly: The Heart of Christ for Sinners and Sufferers* (Wheaton: Crossway, 2020), 19-21.

Chapter 6

Model Mentoring: The Apostle Paul

In this chapter we outline briefly how mentoring was expressed in Paul's life and ministry.

A consistent life

This is where all believers start: 'as He who called you is holy, you also be holy in all your conduct, since it is written, "You shall be holy for I am holy"' (1 Pet. 1:15-16). Farewelling the elders of the Ephesus church where he had worked for three years, Paul referred to his life there and how he had shared the gospel of Christ with everyone (Acts 20:18-35). He had 'coveted no one's silver or gold or apparel'. He was not money-orientated; his life was exemplary. On writing to the Thessalonian church, he declared: 'You are witnesses, and so is God, of how holy, righteous and blameless we were among you...' (1 Thess. 2:10 NIV). Those last words are comprehensive, for his entire life was orientated around loving God, and honouring biblical standards, however difficult his circumstances were. Paul then urged these Christians 'to live lives worthy of God...' (1 Thess. 2:12 NIV). Paul practised what he preached. Wherever he was and whatever happened in his life, he could claim: 'For to me to live is Christ, and to die is gain' (Phil. 1:21). For this reason, Paul reminds Timothy: 'But you have carefully followed my doctrine, manner of life, purpose, faith, longsuffering, love, perseverance, persecutions, afflictions, which happened to me at Antioch, at Iconium, at Lystra – what persecutions I endured. And out of them all the Lord delivered me' (2 Tim. 3:10-11 NKJV). Just as he and his companions modelled consistent God-glorifying lives, so he urged all Christians to do the same, and that must include those who mentor or are mentees. A very important aspect of mentoring is influencing people, by example and persuasion, to pursue appropriate biblical behaviour and priorities. 'The true measure of leadership', wrote John Maxwell, 'is influence – nothing more, nothing less'.[1] That influence is exercised by a life that expresses love, compassion, concern, and seeking the best for a mentee, but without heavy shepherding. Rather than eloquence, learning, or gifts, people respect a leader more for living out what he or she believes and teaches, especially in caring unselfishly for others. Tomorrow's leaders of churches and para-church groups need inspirational and consistent leaders of integrity today. Steven Croft confirms this: 'At the heart of becoming a Christian leader is integrity; a wholeness of life and consistency between the faith we profess and the lives we lead. Integrity is more important than any gifts or skills.'[2] That is thoroughly biblical.

Encouragement

The name 'Barnabas' literally means 'son of encouragement', a nickname given to Barnabas whose name was Joses (Acts 4:36-37). Barnabas was a kind, helpful person who was sacrificial in his service for the Lord. He cared about people so the nickname was appropriate, as he encouraged individuals. Barnabas reassured the suspicious apostles in

---

1. John Maxwell, *The 21 Irrefutable Laws of Leadership,* (Nashville: Thomas Nelson, 1998), 11.

2. Steven Croft, *Ministry in Three Dimensions: Ordinands and Leadership in the Local Church,* (London: Darton, Longman & Todd, 1999), 77.

Jerusalem that Paul's conversion was genuine, so he took the initiative in introducing the former persecutor to them, which was a massive encouragement for Paul. Later, when Barnabas was overwhelmed with the demands of the quickly growing church at Antioch, he travelled to Tarsus 'to seek Saul' (Acts 11:25-26 NKJV) with the purpose of taking him back to Antioch to assist in the work. No wonder that Paul, who had been so encouraged himself by Barnabas, was keen to encourage churches and younger leaders. For Paul, the need to encourage future leaders and assist them in the work was vital.

Gospel

What stands out in the writings of Paul is the importance and glory of the gospel of Christ. He often refers to this gospel in explaining, defending, teaching, applying, and preaching it with joy and zeal. We are not surprised, therefore, that in writing to both Timothy and Titus, this 'glorious gospel of the blessed God', which had been committed to him (1 Tim. 1:11), is at the heart of his theology. He expresses amazement that he himself had become a recipient of the Lord's 'exceedingly abundant' grace in Christ (1 Tim. 1:14 and Titus 3:4-8). No wonder that the apostle bursts out into worship in 1 Timothy 1:17! This gospel was central in what he shared with Titus (1:1-3, 2:11-14 and 3:4-7). Here is an older, experienced leader passing on the gospel to younger men, pressing them to proclaim, teach, and apply this gospel to churches and unbelievers.

Teaching

Reading Paul's letters to young Timothy and to Titus, we see how well he taught them individually in his mentoring of them. Four observations can be made to illustrate the use of teaching in mentoring.

First, both Timothy and Titus had been grounded well in the Bible and its teaching. For example, Timothy had been taught the Bible 'from childhood' (2 Tim. 3:15) by his believing mother and grandmother. Such a grounding in the Bible in the family is important and needs to be re-emphasised today, even in Christian families. An important provision for all, including those lacking the privilege of having Christian parents or other relatives, is the local Bible teaching church. The main preaching and teaching meetings are extremely important and necessary for all Christians. Personal Bible reading is also helpful. Mentoring assumes this background of teaching and familiarity with Bible teaching and in no way replaces it.

Second, mentoring can take potential leaders further by encouraging them to 'hold fast', 'continue', and 'guard' (1 Tim. 6:20) the 'sound words' of Bible doctrines they have been taught. In our contemporary situation key Bible doctrines like the Trinity, the purpose of the Lord's death on the cross, justification, sanctification, or eschatology can be modified in subtle ways so that mentees can require guidance or confirmation in identifying the error in order to 'hold fast' to Bible teaching.

Third, both Timothy and Titus were encouraged to teach the Word by applying it to personal, domestic, church, state, and other pressures. Paul, as a mentor, helped both men in this respect.

Fourth, in writing to Timothy and Titus, Paul was nearing the end of his life and ministry (2 Tim. 4:6-8). There was an age gap here but the challenge for these young men was that soon, and without their mentor, they would be leading churches themselves. The pressures were enormous, for they faced the increasing dangers of heresy, persecution, worldliness, and individuals like Demas and Alexander who had departed from the faith (2 Tim. 4:10, 14). One is not surprised, therefore, that with a note of urgency,

Paul instructs Timothy and Titus to encourage churches in the Word. They need strength and grace themselves for this huge task, so Paul writes that they too must train and mentor others if the churches are to have faithful leaders in the future: 'And the things that you have heard from me among many witnesses, commit these to faithful men who will be able to teach others also' (2 Tim. 2:2).

Relational

For Paul, mentoring was a relationship of love, care, and trust as he developed, guided, and instructed Titus and Timothy, and others. He described Timothy and Titus as 'a true [genuine] son in the faith' (1 Tim. 1:2: Titus 1:4), indicating a close bond existed between them, with Titus probably being one of Paul's converts. Timothy was younger but in need of more care due to his youth, ill-health, and timidity, while Titus was a stronger and more courageous person undaunted, by challenges in church work. Both were key persons as the gospel of Christ progressed into new areas and churches were established. Mentees vary considerably, but what is striking in the Acts and pastoral epistles is Paul's filial relationship with both men as he mentored while working alongside them in ministry. Paul was advising and encouraging them in their varying needs, so his letters to them were strongly relational, breathing an atmosphere of honest realism and care as Paul mentored them. For the apostle, this relational aspect had rich and deep theological significance, pointing to the relationship between the Trinity of Divine Persons in the Godhead – Father, Son, and Holy Spirit. Between them there is perfect love, intimate fellowship, joy, and unity. That profound relational aspect is mirrored in the creation of man in God's image, which includes that of being a social creature. Believers are placed in Christ by the powerful work of the Holy Spirit following regeneration, so the believer is always in Christ, and related to Him and to other believers in one family. Michael Reeves explains that the shape of the Father-Son relationship 'begins a gracious cascade, like a waterfall of love: as the Father is the lover and the head of the Son, so the Son goes out to be the lover and the head of the church.'[3] That intimate relationship of love and kindness needs to be expressed by believers towards one another, and within mentor-mentee relationships as well.

Intentional

There was nothing haphazard about Barnabas's befriending, encouraging, then briefly mentoring Paul; it was intentional. That was true of Paul's mentoring of young leaders like Timothy and Titus. An important question arises here: how can we express this intentionality regarding mentoring? In addition to what has been said earlier, note that Paul identified both Timothy and Titus on his preaching journeys, and became aware of their background and potential. Regarding Timothy, Luke informs us 'he was well spoken of by the brethren who were at Lystra and Iconium' (Acts 16:2). That was a major factor in Paul identifying him, for he stood out in his local situation as a person with potential, and a clear testimony. On that basis, Paul invited Timothy to accompany him on his preaching itinerary, so they became close friends. As they travelled through several cities together, the 'churches were strengthened in the faith, and increased in number greatly' (Acts 16:5). That was a valuable experience for Timothy in witnessing the Lord at work in the churches, and getting to know Paul.

Nourishing

We have seen that fostering care and nourishing is foundational in mentoring, and this was expressed genuinely

---

3. Michael Reeves, *The Good God: Enjoying Father, Son and Spirit,* (Milton Keynes: Paternoster, 2013), 10.

in Paul's ministry. For example, he urged the Corinthian church to respect his authority because 'in Christ Jesus I have begotten you through the gospel' (1 Cor. 4:15). Paul had become their spiritual father, for many of them were converted through his ministry. They may have many instructors, yet not 'many fathers', so Paul urged them to 'imitate me' (v. 16). Paul's emphasis is on Christ, the gospel, and his own role in bringing them to Christ. However, he did not want them to become dependent, for his aim was to nourish and mature them as believers. Paul uses the image of a father, and also of a nursing mother, to describe his love and care for the church at Thessalonica (1 Thess. 2:7,14). The tender language used expresses his aim to nourish and grow believers in Christ. Here again, the relational aspect must express the cascading love of the triune God, so our hearts need to be right with God and captivated by His gospel.

Prayer

This aspect of mentoring has already been referred to, but there is need to underline it in concluding our focus on mentoring by the Lord Jesus Christ and the apostle Paul.

The Lord Jesus himself prayed privately and frequently; the disciples observed Him in prayer, as when He prayed in the Garden (Luke 22:39-46) or on the cross (Luke 23:34,46, Mark 15:34). On one occasion after they had seen Him praying, they requested Him to teach them to pray (Luke 11:1-13). He also prayed specifically for the apostles and all believers (John 17), then urged upon the disciples the necessity of prayer in specific, demanding situations (Matt. 9:37-38, 21:21-22). He prayed for individuals like Peter when Satan sought to ruin his life and witness. Said Jesus, 'I have prayed for you that your faith should not fail' (Luke 22:31-32). However, the essence of prayer for the Lord was intimate fellowship with His Father.

Paul also gave priority to prayer in his life and ministry, as did the other apostles (Acts 6:3-4). He prayed for churches diligently (Rom. 1:9-10; Phil. 1:3-4,9-11; Col. 1:3,9-11; 1 Thess. 1:2-3) and for individuals like Philemon (Philem. 4) and others. Prayer was an integral feature of his ministry, while he enjoyed intimacy with the Lord in prayer (2 Cor. 12:8-10). What is pertinent to our subject is that Paul prayed fervently for those he mentored. He reminded Timothy, for example, that 'without ceasing I remember you in my prayers night and day' (2 Tim. 1:3). All too often this dimension of prayer is weak, rather than central in our lives, so can we address this lack? This is where we begin, for we are losing out on fellowship with our covenant God. Nothing is more thrilling and enjoyable than knowing the presence and fellowship of the Lord (Phil. 3:10). Those who are of most help to Christians are those who spend time in God's presence.

In the next section we will see these principles applied today in the lives of others, and hopefully learn more about mentoring.

Chapter 7

Learning From Others: Megan Conway

We are now meeting Christians who were themselves mentored, and are mentoring others. Megan Conway is the first to share with us.

Megan is from North Wales and graduated from Metropolitan University, Cardiff, and was a UCCFW[1] staff worker in Wales for six years. Now she serves as an evangelist in a local Swansea church sponsored by the Wales Leadership Forum. From a Christian family and a church in Flint where her grandfather was pastor, Megan also benefitted from Evangelical Movement of Wales Christian camps. She has a passion to share the gospel with unbelievers and see Christians maturing in their faith, knowing the Bible, and enjoying the Lord.

Q 1: Being brought up in a Christian family, did relatives mentor you?

A: Both my parents are Christians and I am grateful for their prayers, guidance, and encouragement, even before I became a Christian. They were delighted when I became a Christian as a teenager and, over the years, they encouraged us as children in the faith. They loved their children, so it's impossible to describe the extent of their influence on me over the years.

---

1. Universities and Colleges Christian Fellowship Wales

Q 2: Did other relative/s mentor you?

A: My grandfather was a big influence on me, though I did not recognise it as mentoring at the time. In North Wales, many people do not use the English word 'Grandfather' but the Welsh equivalent 'Taid', pronounced like the English word 'tide'. Taid's influence on me, my sisters, and family has been considerable. After all, Taid was the pastor of our church for years and exercised a fruitful ministry. I learned so much from his teaching and preaching. He never failed on a Sunday to preach Christ crucified, but also taught us about our privileges and responsibilities as Christians to become more Christlike. All the meetings were beneficial, and Taid regularly applied Bible teaching to our lives wisely.

Q 3: Did Taid mentor you too?

A: He did, although he did not use that term. I did not realise what he was doing at the time. Taid mentored me in a relaxed way, without ever explaining what he was doing. He was the person I would go to first if I had questions or a problem concerning the Christian life and the Bible. Taid functioned as a counsellor. He longed for us grandchildren to please the Lord in our lives, so he sent us blogs to help us as Christians. He loved to talk about the Lord. Sometimes he raised topics about the Christian faith to talk about and gave his own input. Taid also emailed and kept in touch, and prayed for me and the family. In many ways, he was an example, a mentor whom I admired and loved. It was a delight to be with him and Nanna, but Taid particularly took initiatives in talking about the Lord and caring for us spiritually.

Q 4: Has Taid continued his mentoring of you?

A: Taid died late in 2019 and I miss him loads, but he was always so strong in faith that I found it encouraging. He knew the Lord deeply and talked about the Lord being 'very real'. His life, his love of Christ, his care of people, but especially his looking forward to being with Christ, has been such a huge challenge to me personally. The text he gave for his funeral sermon was Philippians 1:21: 'For to me to live is Christ, and to die is gain.' That summed up my Taid. He lived and practised what he believed. His influence on my life was profound. I thank the Lord for him.

Q 5: Thank you Megan. Did other relatives mentor you?

A: Certainly, relatives helped and influenced me for good in many ways. I can single out one significant influence on my early Christian life. My cousin's wife, Carys, whom I met initially in a Christian camp before she started courting my cousin, really helped me a lot. Was she mentoring me? Probably she was. For a period of at least two years, we were in touch almost daily. She was an older, stronger Christian, so she texted Bible verses to me on a daily basis and, in this way, I began to learn my way round the Bible. That was helpful. Her passion for Christ and desire to see people saved was infectious. She had a passion for evangelism, and this affected me deeply. I was encouraged by her to memorize Bible verses, which has stood me in good stead, and I still remember those verses. She phoned me often, and would always excitedly tell me about people she had shared the gospel with either at school or outside. I remember her sharing her joy that she had been talking with a lady on a bus and shared the gospel with her. Carys always encouraged me to seize opportunities to share the gospel spontaneously and regularly with friends and strangers. I asked her questions and she gave me helpful answers and advice. She became a kind of big sister and a very good friend, but now she is married and has her own family. I encourage others to do for their friends what Carys did for me.

Q 6: I know you have both discipled and mentored Christians. Can you tell us how you did that?

A: When individuals have seen that I love them and genuinely care about their relationship with the Lord, it has been fairly easy to get alongside younger Christians to encourage and mentor them. There have been brief periods of mentoring, while some relationships have lasted for a few years. This has been helped largely because I was involved as a UCCF Staff Worker.

Q 7: What else has been important in being alongside others and mentoring them?

A: I have learnt the importance of listening to individuals, but really, really listening to them with the aim of trying to understand them, their circumstances, and challenges. Listening has been a key feature in my relationships, and so has being non-judgemental. I have also expressed my love for those I am mentoring by simply giving them time or buying them coffee. This also involves remembering what they have said on previous occasions, and giving them a call in the week to check how they are getting on. They are obvious things to do, but these have been some of the ways in which relationships have grown and developed into influential mentoring type relationships.

Q 8: Are there variations in approaching individuals?

A: Of course. In listening to individuals, there are scenarios in conversation with someone when I may ask a question that really stumps them. It was probably a question that challenged something they had said or believed, so then they want to probe with me and engage in further conversation to understand where I was coming from.

Q 9: Have you an example of this?

A: Here is an example that occurred just when Covid-19 started. I was speaking with one student about the songs he enjoyed listening to in times of what he regarded as 'worship'. I asked who he was worshipping? And what were the songs really saying? I asked too how he knew that the words of the songs were true? This played on his mind. Later we began studying Paul's letter to the Ephesians and discussed its message on several occasions. As a result of this interaction, he has committed his life to the Lord and has been growing tremendously as a Christian. That is thrilling to see.

Q 10: Does any mentoring relationship stand out for you?

A: There have been a few students who have wanted me to be involved in caring for them spiritually and mentoring them. There have been some, over the six years or longer, who have loved to spend time reading God's Word with me, discussing and understanding Bible verses. There is one student who, for the three years of her undergraduate studies, wanted me to encourage and challenge her in the Word, and to point her to the Lord in every kind of situation so she could learn to trust the Lord more. After graduating, she became my relay worker with UCCF for one year alongside another young lady. This was a wonderful year of watching the two girls grow in knowledge of the Lord Jesus and in love for God. Specifically, the four years spent in a close mentoring relationship were tremendous years of growth for her, and encouragement for myself. I remember some of her ideas and fears in her first year, as she had a warped understanding of what Church was and also a great fear of people when considering evangelism. By God's grace, I was able to see her grow and learn; she understands more of the riches of the gospel through our times spent together. It was a privilege to witness her showing another relay worker how to engage in good conversations in evangelism without fearing anyone. She had come a long way and was now passing on her experience to others and training them. She and I continue to be wonderful friends, and I still get a message from her asking my opinion of a Bible text or advice concerning something. This is a continuing relationship, and we both contact one another if there is something to share.

Thank you, Megan, for sharing with us.

Questions:

1. Does Megan's story challenge you? If so, how?
2. Are there specific actions you need to take in the light of Megan's example?

Chapter 8

Learning From Others: Lindsay Brown

Lindsay was born and raised in Merthyr Tydfil in South Wales. He became a Christian at the age of thirteen, then studied Modern European History at Oxford, and later went to Paris to study theology. He served as a staff worker for UCCFW,[1] visiting and encouraging Christian Unions in Wales, then became a staff worker with IFES, and General Secretary from 1991-2007.[2] IFES is a global student ministry linking 500,000 evangelical students together in 160 countries around the world. UCCF is the UK branch of the global work. From 2008 until 2017 Lindsay was the International Director of the Lausanne Movement. For over forty years he has been involved in student ministry and continues to serve as the director of FEUER – the Fellowship of Evangelists in the Universities of Europe. He is married to Ann, whom he first met through the student work in Wales. They have 2 children: Owen, who works with Christians in Sport, and Jessica Angharad, who predeceased them.

---

1. Universities and Colleges Christian Fellowship Wales
2. International Fellowship of Evangelical Students

Q 1: In the light of your wide Christian experience and involvement, are you comfortable with the term 'mentoring'?

A: Yes, if mentoring is the deliberate investment in the spiritual development of other believers, as in the life and ministry of the Lord Jesus exemplified in Luke 8-10. Intentional investment is good, but I am wary of intense investment, which can lead to overdependence on the mentor. The goal of the mentor must be to help the mentee to become a disciple of the Lord Jesus, not of the mentor. I cannot say I was mentored by one individual. I have found that there are many individuals who have influenced me, and from whom I have learned so much.

Q 2: Can you share with us any of the early influences on your life?

A: The person who shaped me most was my maternal grandmother. My grandfather died when I was seven years old, so my parents put me to stay with my 57-year-old grandmother for a brief period, as she was distressed following my grandfather's death. I lived with her for twelve years! I saw my parents daily but I lived alone with 'Nana' until I went to university at 19.

My grandmother was a God-fearing and strong character. She shaped me by sending me to Sunday School, where I was eventually converted. Then, we began to read the Bible together each evening, although she was not converted until eighteen months after me as we read the Bible. She was a humble woman who loved Bible stories. My love of Wales I owe to her. She introduced me to the gospel, and the relative stability of my personality is due to her providing me with a framework for life, a Welsh identity, and with unconditional love. She told me daily that she loved me. She lost her only son in his infancy. On one occasion, she said to me, 'God has been very good to me. I lost my son, so he gave me a grandson to raise.' Her influence on me was profound.

Q 3: Were there other influences on your earlier life?

A: In my youth I can suggest two men in the Merthyr area. One was Raymond Powell: a railway man, the Church Secretary, and Sunday School Superintendent. As soon as I was converted, Ray encouraged me to speak in open-air meetings, even on the challenging Gurnos housing estate (where most of my extended family lived). He also made me a Sunday School teacher at 14, so I memorised the Scriptures as I taught them to 7-year-olds, and learned to be bold through speaking in the open air most weekends. Ray had a great influence on my life. The other person who influenced me was my history teacher in Cyfarthfa secondary school, Mansell Richards. He was the first to introduce me to the sixteenth-century Protestant Reformation and the Reformers who shaped my thinking. He is the finest history teacher I have known ... better than any teacher I heard in Oxford! So, many of my convictions were shaped by the time I left for university.

Q 4: Who influenced you during your studies in Oxford?

A: I became a close friend of Stephen Clark, a fellow Welsh student, who introduced me to quality Christian literature and helped me to think doctrinally, and this relationship has continued over the years. During my period as President of Oxford Christian Union, I had the privilege of hosting each visiting speaker, over twenty-eight weekends, for a meal on Saturday evenings for an hour and a half before the main meeting. The guest speakers included James Packer, Martyn Lloyd-Jones, David Watson, John Stott and Michael Green. I prepared questions beforehand and I learned a lot from them, especially in showing me how to preach, and they did so of course by their different styles of preaching. They must have been exhausted after being questioned so much, but it was an immense privilege to share with them and learn from their experience and public preaching. One weekend, when Martyn Lloyd-Jones was the guest speaker, I was asked to call the Christian Union Committee together on the Sunday afternoon for them to ask him any questions they wanted. That was so beneficial, as we plied 'the Doctor' with many questions for two hours. I remember many of his answers over 40 years later.

The above examples were not deliberate mentoring relationships. However, I worked with some of these men in later years. For example, John Stott was Vice-President of IFES when I was appointed General Secretary in 1991, and he spoke often in our conferences. I visited him many times, so his influence on me was significant. Lloyd-Jones had previously been the founding chairman of IFES. He drew up our doctrinal basis and also invited me to his home for Welsh cakes and discussions – an irresistible combination! I have also worked with Michael Green over 14 years in our vision to evangelise students in European Universities and develop potentially gifted national evangelists. Among those three men, I found Stott to be the clearest exegete of Scripture, Lloyd-Jones to be the greatest preacher, and Michael Green to be the most gifted university evangelist. I learned from all three.

Q 5: Tell us more please about Michael Green's influence on your life.

A: I need to refer back to my student days in Oxford as I begin to answer you. With a few close student friends like Stephen Clark and Gareth Lewis, we began open-air preaching in the centre of Oxford every Saturday during term time. We had not realised that our preaching was aggressive and culturally insensitive in this famous University town. One day, Michael Green, who was the Rector of the large

St Aldgate's church in Oxford, was walking around the town and stopped to listen as we preached. His response was a model of how an older Christian can help younger ones. He saw we were raw and inexperienced and told us: 'I like what you are doing. Can I do it with you?' He then suggested using a microphone (instead of shouting at the top of our voices, which was frightening some people), the use of a few Christian songs, a music group, and also good quality literature. He also suggested that we invited interested people to have free coffee in the church's cafe nearby. Michael Green recognised our passion for the gospel and our gifts but, rather than criticise us for our rawness, he accompanied us and wisely improved what we were doing. That was a huge help and learning experience for us as younger Christians.

Interestingly, like John Stott, I was involved with Michael Green much more in later years when we worked together as evangelists in the Universities of Europe.

Q 6: Please tell us about this collaboration and the Fellowship of European Evangelists.

A: The Fellowship of Evangelists in the Universities of Europe (FEUER) was born out of the IFES focus on evangelism in the student world. At its heart is the desire to find and develop people with gifts of public proclamation across Europe, who are bold in proclaiming the Gospel in a secular context. It has, as its main mission, the determination to winsomely but fearlessly engage in publicly proclaiming the gospel of Christ in the universities of Europe in partnership with evangelical student groups. We do this through seeking to unearth people God has blessed with the gift of public proclamation. When we started, public proclamation only occurred through 5-day Mission or Events weeks in the UK and Germany but, over the last 13 years, with God's help, we have found and developed national evangelists in over 30 of the 40 countries in Europe. We now have a core team of over 70 national evangelists, but about 200 attend our annual conference. We also run national 'Proclama' training programmes for potential evangelists. We never work alone, always in teams; always in partnership with local student groups, and seeking the prayerful support and backing of local churches (into which we seek to introduce those who profess faith). Alongside the public meetings, we also emphasise the importance of equipping students to 'gossip' the gospel and to explain it through gospel-based Bible studies in small groups. Alongside the proclamation we use the visual arts, public testimonies, and music as a means of bridgebuilding and opening the way for the public proclamation. By all these means, and with God's help, before Covid we were able to host Mission/Event weeks in at least 200 Universities annually all across Europe in at least 30 countries each year (during the Covid pandemic, many similar events occurred online). In addition, we run an ongoing mentoring programme aiming to unearth and develop University evangelists. This is done through our annual European conference, where everyone has to give a sample talk that is gently evaluated, through inviting everyone to be involved in a national 'equipping' programme, and participation in at least one Mission week a year, where they can learn from observing an experienced evangelist and working in a supportive team. There are also national training or equipping programmes.

Q 7: Where does Michael Green fit in to this?

A: Thirteen years ago, I asked Michael Green for his help and support in establishing this work in European Universities, as he was an experienced University evangelist. At the time, there were very few university evangelists across the Continent. For several years we both worked together, seeking to evangelise and also identify, then mentor, national evangelists in different countries. Before his death he typically spoke at about six Mission weeks a year (of the 200), but of course the work has grown as God has raised up an increasing number of mature national evangelists, so that today the work is overseen by a team of 12-15 evangelists from across Europe.

Q 8: I know Michael Green's influence was a key factor in developing the work across Europe with you and others. Can you tell us more?

A: He had been leading university missions, especially in the UK, for several decades, had a track record of fruitful evangelistic work, was amazingly bold, and shared the burden for reaching students with the gospel right across Europe. He was especially gifted in the public defence, articulation, and proclamation of the gospel, as well as in building and modelling team-based evangelism. Michael was also most helpful in encouraging young evangelists in removing all jargon and language that would be meaningless to students, while at the same time encouraging them to build the narrative and develop the gospel message clearly. This is a major part of developing young, inexperienced evangelists. He was a great Barnabas to younger evangelists when they had few models to learn from across Europe.

Q 9: You have talked about many influences on your life, but I ask again whether there has been one person you can single out as having mentored you?

A: I hesitate in saying that I had one person with whom I was in a deliberate mentoring relationship. But if the essential requirements of mentoring are spending time with a person, modelling a Christ-like life and setting tasks, then evaluating one's performance as well as providing ongoing encouragement (as Jesus did in Luke 8-10), then I would say that person would be George Verwer. George, the founder and director of Operation Mobilisation, served for many years in its ministry of evangelism, discipleship and church planting worldwide. He has been very significant in my life, especially in my formative 20s. He spent time with me, and took me as his travelling companion for many speaking engagements in a camper van in the Middle East and Scandinavia. During those trips, he asked me many questions and shared what he was reading. His passion for the gospel was immense. His wisdom and extensive reading, together with his passion for the global advance of the gospel, was infectious. He deliberately invested time in me. He came and stayed in our family home, got to know my parents, and came to our wedding. He is a great letter writer, just like the Apostle Paul. He still writes to me and sends books, almost every month! I also spent a formative year on OM's ship, the *MV Logos*, during my first year after graduation, travelling around Africa and engaging in lots of evangelistic work. It was a formative year; I often refer to it as my 'fourth year in the university of life'. It provided wonderful preparation for later ministry, and gave me a global perspective.

Q 10: You must have mentored many Christians over the years, Lindsay. Can you share how you went about mentoring others?

A: While I was a UCCFW staff worker caring for the University and Colleges' Christian Unions in Wales, I was influenced by a book, first published in 1974, entitled *The Master Trainer,* written by P. T. Chandapilla. At the time, Chandapilla was General Secretary of the Union of Evangelical Students of India. (Incidentally, he was a good friend of Lloyd-Jones.) The book challenged me in thinking how to influence young people and care for them as Christian students. Chandapilla had identified key principles from the Gospels concerning our Lord's mentoring of the Apostles. I learned at least three things from the book: the importance of spending time with individuals, modelling a consistent Christ-centred life, and then endeavouring to encourage and also evaluate their service for the Lord – all based on the model of the Lord Jesus Himself. It was all about character-shaping and being with these individuals in developing them in ways pleasing to the Lord and necessary for His work.

Q 11: Can you identify the main ways in which you worked these principles out at the time?
A: I do not claim to be as effective as any of the people I have mentioned, but here are two examples.

First, on each visit to a university or college Christian Union in Wales in the late '70s, I always wanted one hour with each of the Christian Union committee members. This would happen about three times in each of the three terms during the academic year. There were between six and eight persons on a Christian Union committee, so I deliberately spent time with each individual and invested in their lives, spending half the time discussing personal lifestyle matters or questions, and half the time discussing the specific role they had to fulfil as part of the Christian Union leadership team. New committees were elected in March each year. As soon as I knew who they were, I asked them all to join me either on a summer team or a summer church campaign in Wales (we ran between three and six each year), or on an overseas team (usually two each summer). This gave me more time to provide teaching/training, either in a local church context or in a short-term missions' context. Each day on these teams we aimed to spend time (two or three hours divided into three sessions) dealing with a great doctrine, praying around the world, and helping them to be better equipped to answer questions unbelievers ask. I believed it was vital to be intentional, always asking, 'How can I be helpful and an encouragement, not a stumbling block, to this individual, who is made in God's image?' In all this, we tried to mix teaching, modelling, and praxis.

During one summer I took some students with me to L'Abri (French for 'the haven' or 'shelter') in the Swiss Alps where Francis Schaeffer (1912-1984), with his wife Edith, had established a student commune in 1955. This commune was designed as a spiritual oasis for young people with varied intellectual, spiritual, and moral needs, including many disaffected children of missionaries. Schaeffer, a Presbyterian pastor, theologian, and philosopher, handled the questions of young people in L'Abri brilliantly. When students returned to their CUs in Wales in September, they were fired up for Christian witness on campus. Schaeffer was the best answerer of questions I ever saw. He treated questions seriously and demonstrated the defensibility and truth claims of the gospel. God used him to rescue many doubting young people (including many who had grown up in Christian homes!), and gave many a confidence in the trustworthiness of the Gospel, (including my wife of 40 years), for which I am very grateful!

In more recent years, I have tried to identify about 12-15 younger evangelists (mostly in Europe, but also a few in Asia and Africa) in whom to invest. I try to apply some of what I have learned from some of the people I have mentioned above (albeit imperfectly), aiming to meet with them all individually three times a year electronically (by zoom or phone) and at least once face-to-face. I want to withdraw increasingly from organisational leadership, and do more of this kind of investment in the remaining time God gives me to serve Him.

Q 12: Is there anything else you would like to share?

A: On one occasion, a friend and I had tea with Dr Martyn Lloyd-Jones in his London home, which was a formative and unforgettable experience. During our time together, 'the Doctor' urged me to keep up my reading but also to find an older man I could meet with every two or three months to discuss my reading, for this would compel me to continue reading consistently. He told me that many young preachers grow stale because they stop reading, and he encouraged me to contact the Rev. Geraint Fielder (1935-2016), a Presbyterian minister in Abergavenny, Monmouthshire, at the time. I met Geraint and learned a great deal from him as we shared our reading at regular intervals. Geraint never viewed it as a mentoring relationship (he was probably too self-effacing and humble to view himself as a mentor), but he influenced me for good and our friendship continued for years as we attended conferences and travelled overseas together. He was my supervisor when I was a young student worker in Wales, spoke at my wedding, as well as at my daughter's funeral, and was an elder in our church in Cardiff. He was a wonderful, sensitive, godly man, who modelled a desire to see the gospel advanced, even if the advance was led by someone else; a real evangelical statesman.

I have been exceedingly privileged to learn from a range of people, and I am grateful for their influence on my life. In Wales, we have been cautious in the past about learning from only one person. I understand the dangers of obsessively following the example of only one human being, but I think it is good to be hungry to be a lifelong learner, and learn what we can from a wide range of people with different gifts and strengths. That's the beauty of the church.

Thank you, Lindsay, for sharing with us.

Questions:

1. *What impresses you about Lindsay's early Christian life and witness?*
2. *George Verwer's influence on Lindsay and mentoring were invaluable. Are there aspects in that mentoring that you admire and can possibly develop?*

Chapter 9

Learning From Others: Fiona Steward

Fiona Steward is from Ramsey in Cambridgeshire. Her parents are strong Christians and she herself became a Christian in her early teens. Fiona graduated in French at Canterbury University then studied further in France and worked there for a short period. After a call to serve the Lord, she studied theology in Wales in order to prepare for missionary work in France. She was then called to share the gospel with university students in Bordeaux, where she remained for more than eight years. It was a demanding ministry with great challenges as well as remarkable joys. The Lord was faithful to his promise in Acts 18:9-10. Returning home, she accepted a position as Pastoral Lead for women in a large Cardiff church.

Q 1: Becoming a Christian at the age of fourteen, Fiona, did your parents mentor you in your Christian life?

A: Yes, I see them as some of the most important mentors in my life, though they would never call it that.

Q 2: Influence is a major part of mentoring, so can you identify some of these parental influences?

A: Example is one of the greatest teachers. Watching my parents has made me want to follow in their steps. They have always prioritised the means of grace both personally and in their local church, and their lives have borne the fruit of that. What stands out most is their selfless serving of others. They have shown me the importance of availability, grace, and honesty in relationships. They have modelled how to listen well, give wise counsel, and be trustworthy; how to always point to the Lord and His Word, and to pray about everything. What Christ-like encouragers they are! And *that* is a big part of mentoring.

Q 3: Thank you. While your parents mentored you, do you think there are different kinds of mentoring?

A: I have experienced three different types of mentoring, which I distinguish as peer mentoring, professional mentoring, and personal mentoring.

Q 4: OK, so can you describe peer mentoring?

A: This is a mutual mentoring relationship. It has happened naturally but irregularly in my long-standing friendships, but it has been intentional and regular in the small discipleship groups I set up in the student ministry and the church. It can help if there is an affinity, both personally and spiritually, with others in the group. Trust, love, and honesty are essential. It's an informal and intentional way of personally sharing and supporting one another, applying the Word and praying together. This kind of peer mentoring has been a vital tonic and spur in my Christian walk.

Q 5: Can you tell us about professional mentoring?

A: When I began full-time student ministry in Bordeaux, I joined another missionary, Carol Liddiard, who had pioneered the work and gained considerable experience with students. She was preparing to retire and pass the work on to me. She mentored me in a professional capacity but we had a trusting friendship, care and respect for each other too.

Q 6: How did Carol mentor you?

A: Carol mentored me firstly by her life. She was very faithful, whole hearted, and knew God. Her faith made a big impression on me in what was a difficult work. She mentored me as we studied the Bible and prayed together. I will never forget what I learnt from seeing her dependence on the Lord both in His Word, as a lamp to her feet, and in prayer – it *was* the work! Carol also mentored me as we did ministry together. This is one of the best ways to be mentored. I learnt by watching her, by making mistakes and applying her advice. She was so wise and what she taught me impacts me to this day. She was a good mentor in stretching me whilst giving me freedom to be who I was. All of this worked, only because it was done in a context of grace and love. This professional mentoring ended when Carol retired, although we are still in touch from time to time.

Q 7: What about the more personal mentoring you experienced?

A: I have been personally mentored by someone who has had a significant involvement in my life over many years, and is much older than me. Although we never talked about mentoring, in God's providence, it just happened after having known each other for a period of three years. It was based on a mutual concern, respect, and trust. I was struck by the fact that he *really* cared (a rare thing!), knew the Lord deeply in the Word and prayer, and had such wisdom and discernment. I am amazed at his commitment to diligently mentoring me over so many years. This has meant regular contact by email, telephone, and face-to-face meetings whenever possible or necessary. He has always made himself available, even though he's very busy.

Q 8: Are you able to share more details in describing this mentoring?

A: I think it can be summed up as a 'walking alongside'. I am given time. That's important. I am listened to and I feel understood. I am asked probing and discerning questions about my life and my ministry. All is done in a spirit of gentleness and grace, even when things need to be said 'straight.' This provides a context of acceptance and safety to be open and accountable, which is vital. I am counselled and advised in the light of the gospel and the Word, which is applied specifically and pastorally. Everything is prayed about. What I share is remembered and followed-up. I am spurred on to realise my potential and gifts. I also appreciate that the sharing is two-way.

Q 9: Did you feel 'drawn' to the mentor at all?

A: Yes. It is the mentor's example that draws you to want to be mentored by them. But there also has to be a natural connection or 'entente' with that person, which means you can really be yourself with them.

Q 10: What does this personal mentoring relationship mean to you?

A: It has been a life line, not just spiritually but for my whole well-being: an immense support through challenging times, a voice of wisdom in working through important issues, a constant anchoring in Christ, and much more. And that's the point: a healthy mentoring relationship should make you rely more on Christ, not on the mentor. I believe strongly that we all, and especially those in ministry, should have this kind of mentoring relationship. It is a privilege, and has made me want to mentor others in a similar way.

Q 11: Now, I know you have mentored others, so how have you gone about it?

A: It has looked a bit different depending on the type of ministry. In the student ministry in Bordeaux, I had several short-term trainees. At the beginning of each week, we would catch up and share personally. Discussion followed on a chapter of a book on knowing God, the heartbeat of life and ministry (e.g., *The Pursuit of God* by A. W. Tozer, *When I don't desire God* by John Piper). This led to an extended time of prayer together. In the latter years, we would also spend Friday morning and part of the afternoon in personal prayer and fasting. This gave us time and focus to seek God and intercede for many individuals and aspects of the ministry. The battle in the ministry was intense, so we clung to the powerful weapon of prayer. It's surprising how much mentoring happened when we prayed together. At a crucial time in the work, we had a day of prayer, reading the Word, and fasting together, in order to seek the Lord for His direction and for breakthroughs in the hearts of French students. No one was more overjoyed than us to see how God specifically answered those prayers that year! Being immersed in the work together and living our lives alongside each other was a massive part of the mentoring too. Bonds were formed in some of those mentoring relationships, which remain to this day.

Q 12: How do you mentor within a church context?

A: The same principles apply, but the opportunities are different. Firstly, I have been involved in mentoring-type relationships with young Christians who need nurturing. It is important to keep it fairly informal, open and warm, as well as Word-focused, which allows for sharing and discussion. This gives an environment in which to think, learn, and grow in. This is normally limited in time, until there has been some growth and maturity.

It has also been a joy to see how the discipleship groups (mentioned above in Q4) have fostered some really fruitful peer mentoring among the women in my church. About five years ago, I invited any women who were interested to a meeting to explain the purpose and principles of these groups. They consist of two to four women who are committed to meeting regularly: from weekly to monthly. The focus is the Word. Most groups use a book or Bible study guide, which is read in advance and then discussed. The aim is to apply that Word specifically in the context of open sharing and caring relationships. Some women purposely wanted to be with women they didn't know, to encourage wider and more inclusive fellowship.

My longer-term vision in the church is to mentor younger, gifted women for greater usefulness, who can go on to mentor others. This means investing more in some individuals, and giving women more opportunities to teach and share together. There have been some lovely opportunities for this in our bi-monthly women's evenings centred around the Word, testimony, and prayer.

Thank you, Fiona, for sharing your experience with us.

Questions:

1. *What impresses you about the parental and also professional mentoring Fiona received?*
2. *Can you trace the important features in the personal mentoring Fiona has benefited from?*

Chapter 10

Learning From Others: Jeremy Bailey

Jeremy Bailey grew up in a Christian home; his father was a pastor for 38 years in the church he helped to plant in Essex and was called 'Home' to be with Christ in 2000. Jeremy was first aware of the convicting and converting work of God as a child. He taught for a few years before training for the ministry in Wales in the 1980s. He has pastored two churches: the first in Kirby-le-Soken, Essex, before moving to his current church in Aberavon, Port Talbot. He is a husband, father, and grandfather.

Q 1: Can you share with us your personal experience of being mentored?

A: Yes. When I started as a Bible College student in 1987, the word, 'mentor', was not in regular use. Looking back, I realise that a number of men took that role in my life. The first was my father. He was my great example, as he was my Pastor from the time I was four years old. I watched him and later, when he encouraged what he saw was a gift of God in me to preach, I often spoke with him about the ministry and the demands and privileges of being a pastor. The greatest lesson I ever learned from him was when I told him I felt called to the ministry. We were alone and he immediately burst into tears. I could not understand why, but later I understood that there were two reasons: he was deeply saddened to lose my wife, Jenny, and me from the church, as we were active members involved in the church's work; but also, he was aware of all the pain and suffering that would be mine as a pastor. As a father and pastor, he wanted to spare me that. But he knew that it is the Lord who calls, and there was nothing he could do but direct me to the Bible college of his choice, which was ETCW,[1] where his good friend (and mentor!) was a tutor.

Q 2: Who was your second mentor?

A: That was Rev. Alex MacDougall, then Pastor of Trinity Baptist Church, Gloucester. I was sent there for a month in 1989 on placement, as part of my Bible College course. I discovered that Pastor MacDougall was an experienced, generous, and wise servant of God. I determined to learn as much as I could from him. Whilst there, I received confirmation of a call to the pastorate of Kirby-le-Soken Evangelical Church. It became important to me to ask as many questions as I could so that I was as prepared as possible to enter the ministry. Pastor MacDougall took me with him on visits, allowed me to preach, let me sit in on marriage preparation classes, and encouraged me to ask as many questions as I wanted. He showed me his study and explained his system of filing and sermon preparation. One of the greatest lessons I learned was how to cope with 'Blue Mondays.' These are those days a pastor feels like resigning because the pressures of ministry are so great. They often occur on Mondays, so Alex encouraged me to follow his example of keeping a file labelled 'Blue Mondays.' This would contain any letters or cards of encouragement from the congregation, which could be taken out and re-read whenever a Blue Monday occurs. It is a practice I have kept ever since, and it has proved very useful. He also showed me that the telephone is the Pastor's greatest friend when

---

1. Evangelical Theological College of Wales, located in Bryntirion House, Bridgend: it is now known as Union School of Theology.

a member is going into hospital. 'Phone them the night before,' was his advice. I learnt so much in such a short time (the mentoring only lasted a month), but the lessons have lasted a lifetime.

Q 3: Did you have another mentor?

A: My longest serving mentor has been Rev. Andrew Davies. I came under his ministry as a student attending Freeschool Court Evangelical Church in Bridgend. Jenny and I were there for two years, but the friendship lasted for thirty years. Again, the greatest lessons were learnt by example. I listened to the sort of preaching I had never heard before. I was gripped by its logic and power, aware that the voice of God was being heard. I also saw how he handled mid-week Bible Studies and how he pastored people. This encouraged me to keep in touch with him when I became a pastor. Within a few months I hit deep and distressing problems in ministry that drove me almost to despair. It was to Andrew I turned. He was always available and prayed for me regularly. We met up on several visits back to Wales and he took a real interest in me, even to the extent of arranging for me to preach with a view at a church in Wales when things got really difficult in Kirby. The result of that was to confirm in my heart that I was called to Kirby, and I returned there for another 15 years! There was great wisdom in his advice and practical help. Over the years our contact has reduced in frequency, but his influence has only increased. As an example of godly leadership and pastoral care, he has been second to none.

Q 4: What are your main reflections on your experiences of being mentored?

A: Being mentored like this developed naturally from friendships. They were based on an equality of role in the pastorate rather than any sense of superiority on the part of the mentor. No regular meetings were organised; rather it was a case of my need driving me to contact my mentor. What I appreciated most was the availability of the mentor at my point of need, and their willingness to listen to me. Often, they did not offer advice, just a listening ear, a direction to Scripture, and a sharing of their own experience. They drove me to rely upon the Lord, and to remember my calling and the promises of God. The words 'mentor' and 'mentoring' were never used. If anything, I would refer to them as friends and brothers in the Lord.

Q 5: Can you now tell us a little about your experience of being a mentor?

A: My experience with Andrew Davies and Alex MacDougall as mentors has been mirrored in my relationship with one particular friend. He came to us at Aberavon during his training at Wales Evangelical School of Theology (WEST, which is now called Union School of Theology) in an informal placement in his final year. We immediately became good friends. He was a mature man with a young family. They were attending a more charismatic church in the area and were keen to deal respectfully with them, even though they were no longer in sympathy with their doctrinal position. They left there on good terms and came to us. They became members, and he started to look for a pastorate of his own. I saw his inexperience and need for discipling, so our relationship began as it would for any new member: I offered to do one-to-one discipleship classes with him. We followed *The Disciplines of a Godly Man*, a chapter a week, and spent time together praying and chatting. I soon discovered his gifts and was convinced that he was called to preach. He started to serve the church, and it became obvious that he had a pastor's heart for people. He visited and prayed regularly in the prayer meeting. Preaching was a weakness, but he showed great promise and needed opportunities. We gave him these. The church also called him to be an Elder. This was a great help to me personally. We served together for three years before he was called to a pastorate in England.

Q 6: Did you use the word 'mentor' at all?

A: The word 'mentor' was never used. Rather, the relationship was a development of our friendship. Before he went to England, we met together regularly to pray and discuss matters relating to his new charge. After he took up the position, we were regularly on the phone together. Initially, we would speak on a weekly basis. I would always make myself available to him, whatever time of day or night he needed to speak. Again, I would listen to his concerns and try not to give advice. Rather, I would put questions to him and share my own experience where I thought it was helpful. We exchanged emails on matters that needed more thought. I still pray regularly for him. He has been in the ministry for four years now and the need for phone conversations has become less frequent. However, we meet up when we can, and his church is often on my heart.

Q 7: What have been the blessings of mentoring others?

A: The blessings of mentoring are not one way. I have benefitted greatly from our friendship and conversations. He makes me think about my own ministry and examine my motives. His personality is almost the opposite of mine, but he loves the Lord and has a real gift of pastoring and preaching. As is often the case, he has been through a real time of testing in his first years in ministry, but the Lord has sustained him, humbled him, and taught him precious lessons. Often, I have just looked on to see what the Lord is doing, and prayed for him to be helped by the Holy Spirit. It is the greatest privilege to have this sort of relationship with a brother.

Q 8: Your mentoring of others, then, has been variable. Is that correct?

A: I can think of others along the way, during my 32 years of ministry, whom I have mentored in the way you have defined. Most have been just for a short period. In two cases, I had to discourage men from entering the ministry because they were clearly not called. This resulted, in both cases, with a breach of friendship, which was painful, and not deliberately caused by me. I considered it more important to keep them out of the ministry than to preserve our friendship. Perhaps it is this that distinguishes a mentor from a friend. The mentor must always put the work of the Lord before the relationship.

Within the church there are one or two members whom I have helped to become Sunday School teachers or Elders and Deacons. I would not consider this to be mentoring, but the regular work of the pastor.

Thank you, Jeremy, for sharing helpfully with us.

Questions:

1. *Jeremy was mentored by his father and then two pastors over the years. Can you identify reasons why this mentoring was helpful for him?*
2. *Are there lessons you can learn from Jeremy's mentoring of others?*

Chapter 11

Learning From Others: Maureen Wise

Maureen was brought up in London, living there until she was 18, then left for university. She does not remember any Christian influence in her childhood and never went to church or Sunday school. Her father was, in those days, quite anti-religious, and her mother was a lapsed Catholic from the Republic of Ireland. Following University, she became a social worker with experience as a practitioner, trainer, and manager. After becoming a Christian, she travelled extensively in Eastern Europe, at that time behind the 'Iron Curtain'; she developed friendships with Christians living in those countries. In the 1990s she worked in an area in Romania which had experienced a powerful, recent revival, so Maureen saw some effects of that movement of the Spirit of God there. She first went to Moldova in 1998, where the Lord was working powerfully; her work involved teaching in a Bible College and training social workers who, in turn, also became evangelists. The easing of pressures and persecution of Christians by the Communists in the late 1980s was followed by a great movement of God's Spirit in the country when thousands of people were saved. Maureen has researched that revival from its beginnings in 1988 until about 2001, which is probably the most recent revival of the church in Europe. Recently, Maureen retired. You can read some of this background in her exciting book entitled: Celestial Fire: A recent awakening in Eastern Europe *(Bryntirion Press, 2018).*

Q 1: Maureen, can you tell us how you became a Christian?

A: An earnest quest for God started when I was about 16 or 17, which came initially from an awareness that creation was so wonderful that there must be a God. I began reading the Bible on my own at home, and from the beginning knew that it was true and that it was the Word of God. The Lord drew me and I ran to Him! At first, I understood only that the Lord Jesus Christ was the Son of God and the only way to heaven. An understanding of sin and the Cross came some months later, hearing Glyn Owen preach on Psalm 51. I began to tell friends and family that I was born again and a Christian. I knew this to be true from what I was reading in the Bible, but at that stage I had not gone to church.

Q 2: What happened next?

A: I started going to the church nearest to me, which was the Parish church with an evangelical ministry. There, I was loved and nurtured as a very young Christian. It was a splendid grounding to my new faith.

Q 3: How were you called to missionary work?

A: Some months later, I went with a group of young people from that church to the Keswick Convention, and was thrilled to listen to many missionary speakers. I had a sense then that the Lord was preparing a work for me outside the UK. Involvement with Communist Eastern Europe started in my twenties when I visited there at regular intervals, but I was about 40 before I moved to Romania to work training social workers.

Q 4: As a social worker, did you use various types of mentoring?

A: Yes. I have some experience of peer mentoring and personal mentoring, but the vast majority of my experience would be with professional and personal mentoring, including in a Christian context.

Q 5: Can you tell us about your experience of being mentored?

A: Although I was regularly mentored during my professional career, my enduring sense of being personally mentored most memorably and helpfully was during my years as a missionary with UFM Worldwide.[1] I served in Romania and in Moldova, and whilst I was in Moldova, I had visits from UFM staff who observed and participated in the work in which I was involved, and spent time chatting to me there, and when I returned home. The Lord brought me into contact with some choice servants of His. What a great blessing that was and how very privileged I was to spend time with them! Their service was characterised by the kind of self-giving referred to in 2 Corinthians 8:5; 'They first gave themselves to the Lord and then to us by the will of God.' It was no small sacrifice for them to visit and to endure long working hours in a strange culture and a challenging work. They put those inconveniences totally aside and showed a very genuine interest in the work and in what the Lord was doing, they prayed with me (fervently!), they listened to me and my colleagues, they gently advised by articulating their observations, and were a source of constant encouragement to me. The link was regular, and well-informed, and the interest was authentic. I am semi-retired now, but I can still remember some of their comments years later: 'Always bear in mind what will remain of the work if all the Western support were withdrawn;' 'The spiritual tide is much further in here than it is in the UK;' 'What are your retirement plans?'! (That sent me into a confused downward spiral, until I realised how essential the question was.) I should add that the contact has endured past my semi-retirement, and is a source of great blessing to me!

---

1. UFM Worldwide was established in 1931 as an evangelical, inter-denominational mission and currently serves in thirty five countries

Q 6: Will you share about your own mentoring of Christians and potential leaders, please?

A: Certainly. In Romania my main job was teaching in a Bible Institute and training social workers. Strong bonds were formed with many students during those years, to the extent that I am still in contact with a number of them many years later. It happened quite often that individual students would ask to see me outside of class hours and visit my flat. Some unburdened themselves about stressful or perilous home situations; some wanted to discuss their sense of God's call on their lives and how they thought the Lord was leading them; some wanted to talk about a possible future marriage partner, or a multitude of other matters. Many of them were already mature in suffering from their young years. They had experienced sometimes fierce persecution first hand under the previous regime, and they had all known great hardship and poverty. I counted it a great privilege to help them in any way I could, and my soul was enriched by contact with them. I felt it important to make myself available and approachable to make such encounters a possibility.

I used personal examples from my own life when teaching, which probably reduced the – sometimes awesome – gulf between teacher and student. I made sure I had time for individual requests for a meeting and that, when they occurred, the student had my full attention, with all the right verbal and non-verbal cues from me. There was, I think, genuine interest on my part in the student's predicament. God gave me a real love for these students and I think they saw that. Actively listening to them was always the main ingredient, interposed by shifting and developing the subject under discussion, when necessary, through indirect questions, exploration of underlying issues, and challenge and confrontation, when necessary (very particularly when sin was the issue). Usually, we would agree on goals or actions before the next meeting, and we would review progress on attaining these. We would always end in prayer and I followed up with further meetings or enquiries.

Q 7: Do you train some to mentor others?

A: I do. At present, I am training a Moldovan social worker to mentor a Moldovan social work trainee in the context of working for a Christian agency. My practice is to regularly discuss with the social worker how her mentoring sessions with the trainee are going, and to examine preparation, structure, and content with her. The social worker freely discusses encouragements in her mentoring sessions, together with frustrations and lack of progress in certain areas. For example, the trainee in question has a heart commitment to those she is learning to support, is prayerful and keen to learn from her mentor, but outrageously poor at time management, and easily has her confidence knocked by those who are older than her and more experienced. The social worker has made strides with being assertive with the trainee when she needs to be, and setting clear expectations and deadlines. She is achieving a good balance between deserved praise and rebuke, when necessary, without losing the trust of the trainee. Recently I have begun to listen in to their mentoring sessions on zoom. I switch off my video link to reduce the distraction, but they know I am listening and will discuss the outcome with the social worker. Whilst there is inevitably some superficiality to my involvement, it nevertheless provides a useful platform for me to give informed feedback to the social worker.

Q 8: What is your goal in doing this?

A: Our goal is the formation of a worker who will be very well-grounded in applied theoretical knowledge, who will have an integrated view of how the Scriptures apply to tasks undertaken, and who will have a prayerful approach to all the work she does and all the relationships she forms in the course of work. We need to grow workers who 'serve the Lord Christ' and who realise that we will each give an account to Him for how we have served. We are 'epistles … known and read of all men' (2 Cor. 3:2) and we need to understand that others whom we are mentoring will make judgements about our lives, or lack of it. Let us not grow weary of doing good, for in due season we will reap, if we do not give up.' (Gal. 6:9).

Q 9: Have you mentored others in Moldova?

A: Yes, I was part of a newly formed charity in Moldova, which supports adults with disabilities who have previously lived for decades in closed institutions. We have a large staff group who offer direct support to the men and women in our four houses, and my two Moldovan colleagues have been responsible for their mentoring, training, and oversight. The tendency was, and still is to some extent, to replicate the former Soviet model of autocratic oversight. This model is largely about imposing views and demands on others, with little time for listening or enabling expression of failings and weakness. It has been a long, uphill struggle to change this model of operating into one that is not outspokenly condemnatory of mistakes, and that nurtures, rather than punishes, staff when they fail. One of the real helps has been to train up new mentors from scratch with a different set of expectations and perceptions, as well as directly modelling, as often as possible, a much more positive and fruitful way of interacting. Change is happening, although not always as quickly as I would like!

Thank you, Maureen, for sharing with us.

Questions:

1. *Do you understand the different types of mentoring mentioned by Maureen?*
2. *What are your main impressions after reading this chapter?*

Chapter 12

Learning From Others: David Norbury

David Norbury is from Deeside, North Wales. His mother went to a church in Wales and encouraged her son to go also. David became a Christian through two school teachers. One was a religious education teacher, and the other a maths teacher, who organised the school's Christian Union and a local inter-church group. In 1966, the maths teacher arranged a series of evangelistic meetings under the banner of the NYLC.[2] The speaker was to become a professor of medicine. It was through these meetings that David became a Christian. The RE teacher had helped him to overcome many of his scientific doubts about the Christian faith, including the evidence for the resurrection of Christ. The maths teacher encouraged him to read the Bible, attend the local NYLC group, and started him on the way to doing beach missions. David studied science in Bangor University and was active in the Christian Union there. At the end of his postgraduate studies, he obtained his PhD, then taught for several years before being appointed as science advisor to schools in Dyfed. Later he became an assistant director of education as Head of School Improvement in South East Wales.

---

2.   National Young Life Campaign

Q 1: Who was the first Christian to mentor and influence you?

A: It was a while before I was mentored in any consistent way. While a student in Bangor, the Christian Union started a beach mission in Benllech, Anglesey. I joined the team and there I met DF, who was eager to encourage gospel work and witness in North Wales. On leaving University, I began my teaching career in North East Wales, and my friendship with DF developed gradually and very naturally.

Q 2: How did the mentoring relationship develop?

A: As a teacher, I remember the work being extremely demanding. I married Pat and tried to balance work, family, and serving in a local evangelical church. In addition, I was involved in youth work and became a co-leader with DF of the National Young Life Campaign, a Christian movement, in a local branch. Soon, I joined the NYLC National Council. As a result of a desperate shortage of leaders, I became an emergency team leader on United Beach Mission (UBM). Amazingly, they kept me on as a leader since then! In addition to week-to-week planning and leading the local YL with a small committee of young people, DF and I travelled many miles to national meetings of the NYLC and UBM. DF was about fifteen years older than myself and served in a Senior Manager's role in a large organisation. I had a lot to learn about County Councils, schools, communities, church life, and evangelism. As an experienced and senior man, I respected him and wanted to learn from him.

Q 3: Did the mentoring relationship develop naturally?

A: Yes. As our family grew, Pat and I realised we needed a bigger house. A house move was imminent. DF and his wife had moved to their local village church and, eventually, we relocated and settled in the same village, and went to the same local church. Pat and I settled in, supported the church, and a team, including DF and myself, emerged. We worked well together and, over a period of seven years, we saw the church numbers expand significantly with many, including families, being converted. It became a genuine community church. We learned so much, especially from our mistakes. DF remained a good friend and mentor throughout.

Q 4: How did DF mentor and help you?

A: Looking back, he helped me in several significant ways. He helped in my professional career by giving invaluable advice and encouragement from his management experience. There were pressures in school, challenging bosses, and sometimes tense situations. Coming from the culture of a university to a large, developing comprehensive school was a culture shock! I had to learn – and quickly. How was I to cope in school, at home, and as a Christian seeking to reach out in whatever ways were wise and effective? He was a major help to me; his mentoring influenced my career positively. I had a lot to learn about career pathways too, and to understand God's hand of guidance. DF helped prepare me professionally for more senior levels of responsibility in education. He also encouraged me by stretching me with a wide range of projects in church and YL.

Q 5: Did DF put pressure on you to act as he wanted?

A: Not at all. He was wise, encouraging, and challenging, but did not push me to do anything. The decision was mine, always. In this respect, DF knew his own limitations, and sought to recognise what God was doing in a person's life or in a situation. He was aware of the abilities that I had and also some of the weaknesses. In many of the long car journeys we made to meetings, he encouraged me to be sensible and wise in all I did. He was a man who cared, and was interested in my Christian life and witness.

Q 6: In which other ways did DF influence and mentor you?

A: Apart from our personal relationship, working together in a local church and in area youth work, DF helped me enormously by introducing me to a network of dedicated Christians nationwide. In this respect, he was visionary, and was aware that I needed to mix with Christians from other parts of the country and be involved with, and learn from them in gospel work. Gospel witness was often better caught than taught! He introduced me to UBM, whilst Pat also drew me into the EMW,[1] particularly to my first EMW Camps for children and young people. In this network, I met other godly, loving Christians from different areas. I was blessed, and learned a great deal from these dedicated, sacrificially-living believers; they challenged me enormously in so many important ways.

Q 7: Do you want to say anything else about DF's mentoring?

A: His humility, life example of service, and willingness to admit mistakes, work collaboratively, and listen, were very important. I respected him and warmed to him for those reasons, knowing, too, he cared for people like myself. He also prayed for me. His passion for evangelism and encouragement for me to be involved regularly in evangelism was formative in those years. DF's strengths were not so much in personal evangelism, but rather in thinking strategically, encouraging and planning outreach activities to reach out to unbelievers.

DF gave me a perspective on my working life and Christian service that I could never have known. In the years following, God was to give me other people, and sources of wisdom and perspective, which would build on the lessons God had taught me through DF. In the years

---

1. Evangelical Mission to Wales

that followed, it seemed natural for me to want to share my learning and tailor my support in ways that reflect my extremely positive experiences. DF died recently, but I thank God for his influence in my life.

Q 8: You have mentored others over the years, so would you like to tell us about that?

A: I have been privileged to have been mentored, and also to mentor others. Quality mentoring is desperately needed amongst Christians, particularly for preparing future leaders. Those I have mentored do come back to me – some occasionally and others at regular intervals – so the relationships continue. Normally, these friends are those I met on UBM beach missions or in EMW youth camps. I felt an affinity with them, and our relationship developed naturally. We were on a journey together and I wanted the best spiritually for them, for whatever organisation we were jointly serving, and for myself. I wanted them to understand themselves and their potential better.

Q 9: What form did your mentoring take?

A: I knew I was a servant of the Lord, so I sought to mentor and care for individuals with a servant-like attitude. I avoided a controlling attitude, and did not expect anyone to be my clone. There was no heavy shepherding in commanding people to do what I wanted. My heart's desire was for each mentee to feel safe in the relationship, to know they could trust me and they could rely on me. I wanted to be there for them when they needed my support and encouragement. My overall longing was that they should blossom as Christians, using their lives and gifts to honour the Lord Jesus Christ.

Q 10: Have you mentored within your family too?

A: Certainly, and that has been a wonderful privilege. My wife and I have three sons; each one has become a Christian in the Lord's gracious providence. We are so grateful that they are the Lord's, and seeking to live for Him. I never used the term 'mentoring' in relation to my children, but that is what I aimed to do – and still do – by nudging and encouraging. I tried to avoid interfering in their lives, instead influencing them in the context of a loving, godly home where Christ was Lord. Example, care, listening, being available, and being patient have been some of the qualities I have tried to express in mentoring them over the years. We learn from our many mistakes too. In their own way, they still come back to me for advice on key issues when they feel they need help or direction. In all my mentoring, whether with relatives or not, I have endeavoured to support, encourage, care, motivate, inspire, but also enthuse over the gospel, encouraging them to do likewise.

Q 11: Which age groups ought to be involved in mentoring?

A: Some suggest that those in their sixties can exercise greater influence but the important factor, rather than whether a person is younger or older, is that he or she is a reliable, consistent, faithful servant example to others, with a passion to love and serve Christ. Again, love, care, trust, and a servant-like attitude are essential, whatever the age of the mentor.

Thank you, Dave, for what you have shared.

Questions:

1. *DF's mentoring of Dave over several years began naturally and developed gradually. Are there features in this mentoring that are important for you?*
2. *How important is it to have an affinity with those who mentor us?*
3. *Do other aspects of what Dave has shared impress or challenge you personally?*

Chapter 13

Learning From Others: John-Mark Teeuwen

John-Mark Teeuwen is married to Rosalind, who has a Guyanese/Trinidadian background. Rosalind works in a secondary school with young people who have special needs. They live in Wiltshire and have two adult children. John-Mark was born in Papua, Indonesia, where his parents served as pioneer missionaries with the Dani people. John-Mark has extensive experience in Christian work, having served in pastoral ministry and also in leadership with the UFM Worldwide mission agency. More recently, until August 2022, he worked in England in UCCF student ministry as a regional Team Leader.

Q 1: What place does parental mentoring have for you?

A: I distinguish between parenting and mentoring, and suggest that parenting takes place in the early years and then, as children become older and more independent, although a certain amount of parenting continues, the relationship moves more into one of mentoring. At that stage the children can, and often do, begin to mentor the parents as well. A lot of this depends on the quality of the relationship between parents and children.

Q 2: What kinds of mentoring have you known?

A: I like to emphasise three kinds of friend/colleague mentors:

- Those who are older than me, in which case the mentoring environment has felt more like a respectful relationship of teaching and learning.
- Those who are my own age, and the mentoring has worked best when there has been an atmosphere of trust and friendship.
- Those younger than me, in which case the sense of me being mentored by them has been more organic, and more initiated/led by me. What I mean is that I tend to be inspired by them and therefore choose to learn from them. Most of the time that is unspoken, but there will be times when I ask for their input/insight/perspective, etc.

I have experienced situations where friends/colleagues have been in a position to mentor me, as above, but it has not worked well, often because there is a sense of a lack of engagement, and no clear and deep sense of relating to each other. Sometimes, there can be a sense in which the frameworks being used, whether doctrinal or organisational, become more important than the person.

Q 3: How do you encourage mentoring?

A: This is quite hard but I suggest three things:

- It is good for a church community/organisation to encourage and nurture a culture of mentoring/discipleship in what is spoken, written, and modelled.
- I would want to try to encourage those who are shy to take the step of approaching someone. This is often a complex and slow process, though important, and it needs our constant and wise attention.

- To encourage those who are in a place to offer
  mentoring to be proactive in approaching those who
  might not come to mind in the first instance, including
  those who are shy and perhaps seem unwilling at first
  to be mentored.

Q 4: What about the place of Scripture in mentoring?

A: One example in relation to Scripture is in a situation
where, for example, a mentee helps you to see the deeper
meaning of Scripture or how the way one was viewing God/
Scripture was inadequate.

I remember being helped, and continue to be helped,
by someone explaining the story of Elijah in 1 Kings 19.
What I found especially helpful was how they explained
what seemed to have happened in the interaction between
the Lord and Elijah when Elijah was in the cave – things
like the background to this event; the impact it would have
had on Elijah; the fact he was in a cave, possibly the same
cave Moses was in (Ex. 32); that the Word of the Lord came
to him in the form of a question, not in the earthquake,
wind, or fire, but in the 'sound of silence'. The latter was
especially helpful to me that, in the situation Elijah was
in, he was shaped by a question (repeated at the end) and
silence. The silence made a huge impression on me and has
helped to shape my understanding of Scripture and my own
discipleship.

Someone helped me see something in Scripture that I
hadn't seen before, and it had a deep sense of resonance
with my situation. This is the kind of situation where we see
more clearly that the Holy Spirit is at work, illuminating the
Scriptures and Christ in our situations. The Lord can use a
mentor or a mentee in such cases. Although sometimes the
impact of Scripture is less obvious and noticeable, the impact
of the Holy Spirit through both are constantly impacting us
for God's glory and our 'good'.

Q 5: Can mentoring be brief as well as long-term?

A: Yes, I think there are contexts that create a more short-term mentoring relationship. Sometimes there can even be a one-off conversation/meeting. I can think of examples I had at the UCCF Forum, where the person you are speaking to seems keen to go quite deep, and quickly so, into sharing. These kinds of situations are sometimes referred to as 'low hanging fruit', settings where it seems so clear that the person is in exactly the right place to be sharing in that moment. These can be incredibly brief but very significant moments of mentoring.

Q 6: What are the contexts in which you mentor?

A: This tends to be in the context of the ministry I am involved in and the priorities I am faced with in that situation. I have had a number of situations where people in other contexts have asked to be mentored. I have usually agreed, but find it is often less straightforward because they are not a direct part of the 'natural' setting/movement of life and ministry at that point. I hope this does not sound strange but, in recent years, I get the feeling that all I do is mentoring. That seems to be one way of summing up what I am most busy with and what I naturally gravitate towards.

Q 7: Have you anything else to add?

A: I am not sure what to add, and that comes from a position of being convinced about the Lordship of Christ and His place in everything in everyone's life. This involves acknowledging the reality that each person is made in the image of God, and either needs Christ or needs more of Christ. If I am involved with that person or in that situation, then my own life/perspective has a role to play in the interaction. There are dangers to this approach and it can end up taking a lot of time, and that is something I tend to need, but it has its disadvantages. It can also lead to an unhelpful dependency, at times, as well as an unhelpful level of engagement.

Q 8: Tell us more about mentoring students.

A: This tends to happen naturally, but students are quite proactive these days, open/transparent, and often ask to be mentored, even if it is only for a few meetings or about a particular life situation or theological issue. I enjoy mentoring students!

Q 9: How can we encourage more mentoring?

A: It would be good to nurture an environment where there is more mentoring, which could be formal or informal. At the risk of generalising, I suggest there are some areas we need to explore further as a matter of urgency:

- There is a profound need, in society but also in church, to rediscover the value and experience of true friendship and relationships. I gave a brief talk on this at Forum, and was surprised by the positive response from the students and staff. They all seemed so thirsty for this!
- English and UK evangelical culture functions with certain barriers that prevent a culture of mentoring/friendship and these need to be explored with a view to change.
- Positively, the New Testament community, and many other cultural or multi-cultural communities, are way ahead of us in creating and living in communities that are more geared towards relationships/friendships that involve or could involve mentoring. These could be paradigms for us and instructive.

Thank you, John-Mark, for sharing your thoughts and experience concerning mentoring.

Questions:

1. *Consider further the role of parenting and mentoring.*
2. *How can we encourage more genuine friendships and Christ-honouring relationships in our churches and Christian groups?*
3. *How can we be available to others yet avoid an unhelpful dependency at times, as well as an unnecessary level of engagement with an individual?*

Chapter 14

Learning From Others: Dawid Koziol and Steve Levy

In this chapter it is my privilege to introduce you to two more Christians involved in the Lord's work. This time, however, I am not interviewing them. They will each share briefly their own story, and experience of being mentored and mentoring others.

Dawid Koziol is a young pastor in Zywiec, Poland and is married to Agnieszka. He is linked with the European Mission Fellowship. We see again that servants of the Lord who have served the Lord for many years have considerable pastoral and evangelistic experience, which they can share profitably with younger Christians who are entering, or have recently entered, the Lord's work. Those also serving the Lord voluntarily in Christian service, while occupied in secular work and family responsibilities, can also learn from older Christians.

Dawid writes:
'God, in His providence and grace, shapes us so that we can carry out the task for which He has assigned us. In my case, He used my uncle, missionary, pastor, evangelist Henryk Karzelek. As a young pastor I needed a good example, encouragement and words of wisdom from an experienced worker. God graciously granted it by using Henryk. When I

look back, I can see it clearly. Because of family relationships, the Lord allowed me to look at his family and ministry and just stand and see the qualities of a mature leader. At that time, I was still a teenager.

Henryk was also watching me. It always amazed me that he did not ignore young people; he devoted his time, wanted to talk, listen to us – we who had little to say, although we thought we knew everything. It is difficult to count how many camps we were on together, but it was there that I noticed that Henryk started to give me some responsibilities. These were small steps, little responsibility, that grew over the time. I always felt safe knowing he was standing behind me ready to help and serve with his advice, giving some tips, or giving constructive criticism. He encouraged me to learn and was clearly encouraged to hear that I was going to a Bible school.

It was a great blessing to me to work with him over two years after completing theological training in Wodzislaw and Jastrzebie Church. It was at that time I have learned many practical lessons of pastoral work. Then when I started my ministry in Zywiec (where I am at the moment), I felt I was swimming in the deep waters but always felt and knew, and still do, that Henryk is very much interested in my ministry, in a sense holding the line, always ready to hear and serve me in the time of difficulties and discouragements.

Being a young man and young pastor, I am blessed to find a good example, encouragement, and word of wisdom in one man, in pastor Henryk. Yes, it is by God's grace that we are who we are, by His grace we stand, without Christ we can do nothing, but I can say with conviction that by His grace He put my uncle in my way. Praise God for those who run ahead, clearing the road a little bit, to make it easier for us. Praise the Lord for those who run ahead but sometimes look back to help those who run behind them. The apostle Paul wrote also that we don't have many fathers (1 Cor. 4:15) so we should praise the Lord for the spiritual fathers that He gives us.'[1]

* * *

Steve Levy is the next person to share his experience with us. He has Christian parents and was brought up in South Wales, and currently serves as Pastor in Mount Pleasant Baptist Church, Swansea.

Steve writes:
'As I sat back and thought about mentoring, if I was asked when I was younger, I think I would have listed preachers and their influence but as time has moved on, and with a better perspective, I realize it was others who have influenced me more.

Without doubt number one is my mother. Long chats on wide-ranging subjects of theology, church life and then her great love for the Lord and us children. The fact that she has prayed for me every day of my life, the way she loves to laugh at the ridiculous, all had an influence like no one else. The older I get the more I can see it. Even now she will ask a question about something that we have done as a church and without any other comment I know exactly what she is thinking.

The next place of mentoring was the church I grew up in. There was a huge love of theology, especially the Reformers and Puritans. They read these books and would discuss them with you. They were obsessed with truth and would debate, discuss and encourage, even in my teenage years. I was far from easy, but I knew I was loved in church. What an unseen impact that made. These were the people who went to the prayer meeting and prayed for me and with me and cared for me, invited me into their homes and put up with my questions. They were willing to shoot me down in flames

---

1. Reprinted with permission from Vision, May 2021.

when I was growing up. There really was no room for sloppy thinking. My love for church stemmed from the Scriptures and then seeing it lived out in front of me. That has been the most important foundation.

In the church plant, other members' love; correction from men, but particularly women in the church; to love the lost made a huge impact and saved me from settling for a lukewarm faith; prayers in prayer meetings; chats over coffee or in the home; also seeing believers suffer and die. How they mentor you in growth, in grace. Older believers who have distilled truth down so that they can give corrections or encouragements at just the right time. I still remember Cliff, an old member, realizing I was wavering on the truth. He took me by the arm into the corridor and gave me the most loving dressing-down of my life. Now is just the same. I have spent so much time teaching the children of the church catechisms over Zoom. They have taught me so much about how to love Scripture, zeal, simple faith. There are no words I can use to express these things. As much as I have been helped it is church that the Lord has used to help me grow and it is still church that helps me now. I wouldn't swap one of them for Calvin or Luther or Spurgeon, because the Lord has chosen them for me, to mentor me.

Included in that is the former pastor of the church where I am now the pastor, Clem Roberts and his wife Meryl. They would always have time to just chat. Meryl is now with the Lord. They were larger than life characters, but always supportive and kind beyond expression. I would sit and they would tell stories and then make very kind and helpful observations. On one occasion, I had to speak to Clem about an issue we didn't agree on. He was so kind and gracious, and said he would speak about it again. There were other occasions when they gently pointed out if they thought I was making a mistake. This was very rare and always when I asked. I have to say on the occasions I didn't listen, it always proved to be a massive mistake which I would live to regret. He always told me he was praying for me, which has meant so much to me personally because I know he is. He would call me 'his pastor', I don't know why, but that encouraged me beyond measure. There was one service where it would have been easy to not mention me at all, there was quite a degree of hostility. Over and over again he called me 'my pastor'. By the end I don't think I have ever felt so loved. People say former pastors can be difficult. He was my mentor.

As far as my early experience goes my pastor Paul Tucker was the greatest mentor. I was his milkman and on Friday afternoon I would sit and chat to him. His wisdom was immense. He seemed to have a real ability to change how I thought without me realizing it. I think a key part was spending time with me, and his very gentle and kind way of speaking. He was a great laugh. He taught me the importance of listening and learning from Christians of a wide perspective; over the years this has proved critical in helping me. It was his listening and gentle encouragement and correction, also a desire to push me to think in new ways, which still stands me in good stead. Looking back, his grasp of biblical theology was breathtaking. He would also be quite vulnerable, willing to say things that were quite out there, such as: should preaching be done sitting down? – after all Jesus did it that way. He had different ways of thinking about prayer meeting, and he always laughed at his own mistakes. At the time I barely showed him how much I appreciated him, but his influence continues. Even now I think of his advice.

At this time of my ministry, I see the desperate need for mentors. Even though as you get older the needs change, older men who are wiser to give counsel are a huge help. I have one retired minister I often ring who has strong convictions and will challenge me if he thinks I am wrong.

I find that enormously helpful. I have another retired minister who is gentler, makes me laugh a lot, and yet I find his influence is also great as he gently nudges me to think things through.

One mentor who really opened my eyes is Sam Ko. Apart from the enormous work he has done to help church plants he has taken me to Eastern Europe, Ethiopia and Ghana and what he has shown is that we go to learn, not to assume the West knows best. Listen first. Sometimes all you should do is listen. So much I heard about Christianity is at best patronizing and at worst, just racist. Whereas Sam's gentle advice and desire to teach me to learn first has opened my eyes to see, in each of these countries, things that I would never have learnt at home, and shown huge weakness in western Christianity. It is a joy to know all over the world the gospel is being preached and we all have much to learn from each other.

I have also had the experience of looking to someone for help and then them letting me down, hearing things they were saying which they had never said to me. I am sure there was good reason but I did feel very let down at the time and for quite a while felt I couldn't trust people. People you pray with and worship with are the ones who the Lord gives to help.

There are others who are contemporaries. I love people who have a sharper mind than myself and stretch me. One minister of a larger church is very straight and has helped me see huge blind spots in how I pastor the church. It really is the case of keeping a wide variety of opinions, all with the view that I would be the best servant of Christ I can be for the people the Lord has called me to in Mount.

I never have seen myself in that role so we set up a conference called the Eccentrics, so younger men in the ministry would be introduced to older men with different perspectives. I think some have found mentors there.

Those the church has sent out into the ministry would say there have been a number of influences on their lives, but I myself have tried to show them what has been a blessing to me, encourage them to listen to others of a different perspective, find two or three others to give advice. My weakness, I realize, is that I'm not that great a 'chatter' which is a real gift when you mentor others.

My advice would be, always have someone who loves church and serves in church. There are many who still want to influence and lead others but have no desire to serve others in day-to-day church life. They were around in Bible times and are still around today. I asked Richard Bewes what advice he would give to the young men we are sending into the ministry. 'Prepare for a life of rearranging chairs!' And so it is – a life of simply being a servant in church life.

Questions:

1. *The influence of close relatives is referred to as being significant and helpful, in these examples. How can we try to influence our families wisely and prayerfully?*
2. *Paul Tucker was the greatest mentor in Steve's life. What were the features of that mentoring relationship that were so helpful?*

Chapter 15

Roger Carswell: Investing in Others

Roger Carswell is an evangelist based in the heart of the Yorkshire Dales. He leads evangelistic missions in churches and universities. He loves talking with people about the gospel, he has authored 17 books, scores of tracts and booklets, and often hosts the evangelistic programme Real Lives (www.reallives.net). He is married to Dot, and has four children and ten grandchildren.

Roger writes:
One of the formative books I read as a student was *Daws*, the biography of Dawson Trotman, founder of the Navigators. Even the Apostle Paul didn't write with such long sentences as are found in this book(!), but the other abiding impression was Dawson Trotman's total commitment to reproduce his biblical principles and active service in others. Famously, he wrote a must-read booklet called 'Born to Reproduce'.

He saw four generations of Christians in 2 Timothy 2:2, 'And the things that you have heard from me [1] among many witnesses [2], commit these to faithful men [3] who will be able to teach others [4] also.' Timothy may not have been a natural evangelist, so it is pertinent that even he was instructed to do the work of the evangelist, and part of that work was training another generation to proclaim the gospel. In fact, in Ephesians it is expressly written that part of the ministry of those who are evangelists is 'the equipping

111

of the saints for ministry for the edifying of the body of Christ' (Eph. 4:12).

Aged 15, I had been led to the Lord by my uncle, whilst holidaying with Christian relatives in the Lebanon. Back home in Yorkshire, it took months before I was 'found' by a vibrant gospel-hearted, inter-church youth group in Leeds. It was led by Verna Wright, Professor of Rheumatology at Leeds University. Though we didn't use the word back then, he mentored me. To this day, I have never met anyone with such evangelistic zeal as he. He was a leading academic, a doctor, an elder of a large church, a husband, and father of nine children. Three times a week he would preach at open air meetings in the centre of Leeds; and would also organise a host of regular events to reach out with the gospel. But he had time for me too! He took me under his wing. I had meals with his family. When he was preaching, he would take me and other young people along 'to give your testimony'. He encouraged me to go on beach missions. He would chat with me about my Bible readings and prayer life, as well as help me to grow in evangelistic endeavour. It appeared that that young, mischievous teenager was never too much trouble for him.

And yet, he never lorded it over me. His care for me and input into my life were not dependent upon me agreeing with him, or doing what he said. He was patient, and sought to develop Christ-likeness in my personality, rather than make me a clone of himself. No matter how I might have tried, I could never have become him, but he didn't try to make me a replica of himself. I learned from him, and still feel deeply indebted to him. What I now see he did for me, he was doing with many others, including his own children. He was investing his life in others.

Significantly, his mentoring was not part of his 'job description'. He did not write an hour's appointment in his week's schedule to have a Bible study with me. All his investment into my life, and that of many others, came as a result of his Christian commitment. It was part of the overflow of his life to teach others. The numerous meals his wife prepared, the hospitality offered to so many in his home, and his encouragement to those far less able than himself to lead in the Lord's work left an abiding impression.

Very early on in my full-time Christian ministry, I had the privilege of giving the communion service message at a conference at which Warren Wiersbe was preaching. He was a voracious reader, prolific writer (he wrote 176 books), and director of a huge radio ministry in the USA. But as well, he mentored me as, for over 30 years, he regularly wrote to me, phoned me, came and stayed with my wife and me, and invited us to stay with him and his wife. He introduced me to books to read, and later to book publishers for my own writing, in which he encouraged me. I am sure that both he and Prof. Verna Wright felt I could have done better in many ways, but they never said it, and I thank God for them, and miss them both.

Evangelists are often mavericks, and mavericks make the ministry. Because of the unique calling of the evangelist, they will have to be tough-skinned. Evangelists are often unappreciated and criticised. They will often have to bear the brunt of the disappointment of being let down by fellow believers. Yet evangelists are driven; they are people of passion. They know that the Great Commission is not about debating theology over a latte, or spending the best hours of each day keeping up with administration or sitting on several committees. The evangelist will want to reach lost men and women with the gospel and, if that isn't happening each day, there will be a fire in their bones to change the situation. Evangelists have something to tell, and they must tell it!

But evangelists must not succumb to the temptation to be loners. We should do our best to avoid being seen as either

113

– or maybe both – uniquely gifted or oddballs! Investing in others, equipping the saints, and mentoring individuals, will all help to normalise us, as well as increase our effectiveness. Aesop's famous fable of the wind and the sun wagering each other as to which could make the lone walker take off his winter coat has great wisdom. The harsh wind had the opposite effect to the warm sun. Harsh criticism is not the way to mentor. Mentoring is not manufacturing. The mentor must not strive or be known for his anger or his aggression, but his gentleness and faithfulness. A prayerful person will not scheme and manipulate but, believing that the Lord is the best Mentor, will pray and be patient, allowing the Lord the time to graciously smooth out the rough edges of a person.

In my early years as a travelling evangelist, I would have one young man for (usually) a year to travel with me and share as much as possible in the work of evangelism. It was costly in that I was with them 24/7, week in, week out. I spent more time with them than I did with my wife or children. I don't remember any fallout, and we had great fun together. Several have gone into full-time Christian ministry. With some, but not all, we have stayed in good contact. Altogether there were 17. One of them has renounced his Christian faith, but maybe he joined me more because his parents wanted him to than because of his own conviction. Each had different abilities and strengths, but I did find myself very drained by constantly being 'on duty'. More recently, individuals have been with me on evangelistic missions for just a week or two, and I try to impart what I can, but clearly time and opportunity to talk and teach are limited.

I'm often asked how does a Christian have, and develop, evangelistic passion. There are many ways to answer that, but it is key to be involved with people who are burdened to reach the lost, and are actively evangelising. Passion for souls rubs off! And there is such great joy in explaining the gospel to people – even leading an individual to Christ. With a small group of other evangelists, we regularly hold 'Go Days', where we are reaching people on the streets. We invite Christians from many churches in an area to join us. Then, starting with ten minutes in the Scriptures, followed by prayers, each one decides to join a group either preaching in the open air, doing door-to-door work, distributing tracts, or looking after a free book table. Of course, we are reaching men and women with the gospel, but more than that, we are involving and training people in evangelism. We stress to each one involved that Jesus told us that the message we are to be proclaiming is to be found in Luke 24:46-47 – namely Jesus suffering for our sin; His resurrection; our need for repentance; and to receive forgiveness of sin. As a result of doing the Go Days, some have caught the vision and are organising regular events in their hometowns.

I am linked to a small group of full-time evangelists who work in different parts of the UK, and who specialise in reaching different types of people. Each of us was aware of other evangelists working either in lonely situations or with other organisations. We knew, too, of young people who were considering how best to fulfil their evangelistic ministry. We devised 'The F.E.W.' (Fellowship of Evangelistic Workers). We have monthly contact with them, a weekly Zoom training course in evangelism, occasional gatherings, and an annual conference. These have become very precious times, where evangelists encourage fellow evangelists. Evangelism can be a lonely work, often misunderstood even within churches. Yet I am convinced that the greatest act of kindness I can show anyone is to introduce them to Christ, and the greatest act of tyranny is to know the gospel and yet not share it. If I can influence others to be involved in this work, which is close to the heart of God, then it must make sense. I am not omniscient or omnipresent, so they may go where I cannot. I am not immortal, so they may be able to continue the work when I am in glory. I am me, and they can reach people who are more like them than I am!

I love the old song, 'Every person in every nation, in each succeeding generation has the right to hear the news that Christ can save.' Yes, I want everyone to hear and understand the words, 'Christ died for our sins, was buried and rose again on the third day.' But I am just one person, living in one small place, having a very limited capacity to reach my own 'world'. But, if I can mentor someone else to reach the lost, and they could mentor another, the mission field begins to expand, and the possibility of reaching it becomes a little less daunting.

Pray as to who you could be impacting with evangelistic fervour and skill. Allow the Holy Spirit Himself to guide you to cross paths with someone who, as Dawson Trotman used to say, is F.A.T. – faithful, able, and teachable. They will be showing a desire and commitment to get involved in evangelism. Their prayers will exhibit a burden for lost men and women. Then make yourself available by giving time. Patiently encourage them, prayerfully give them to the Lord, and praise Him if they are able to do greater exploits than you! Of course, there will be disappointments and heartaches, but it may be that the Lord will work with you to mould another worker in a vineyard where fruit is ripe, ready to reap, or to rot.

Questions:

1. *Ponder the influence of Professor Verna Wright in mentoring Roger.*

2. *How does one 'develop evangelistic passion'?*

3. *What is your response to Roger Carswell's mentoring of evangelists? Are there features you need to experience yourself or offer to others?*

Chapter 16

An Urgent Call for Action

A very big thank-you to Megan, Lindsay, Fiona, Jeremy, Maureen, Dave, John-Mark, David Koziol, Steve, and Roger for sharing their personal experiences of mentoring in chapters seven to fifteen. Their contributions are invaluable in giving us excellent examples of mentoring and wise suggestions for developing relational care and support for Christians in churches, Christian Unions, and other Christian organisations.

What can I say in this closing chapter? I have wrestled with that question, and had initially decided to end the book with Roger's moving testimony. However, I continued to question this decision and wrote a draft chapter, then filed it in case I changed my mind. Recently, it has been suggested that I need to include a closing chapter, if only to pin-point ways forward for ourselves in encouraging mentoring. I now accept that suggestion. In essence, this final chapter is an urgent call for action – action that can make a real difference for younger Christians eager to serve the Lord, and to do so even better. My way of doing this, therefore, is to underline some key principles found in the testimonies in chapters seven to fifteen, and then add my final thoughts as well as suggestions for Further Reading.

Family

I am encouraged by references made by several contributors to parents, grandparents, and an uncle who mentored them so helpfully. In our fragmented society, with many broken and dysfunctional families, it is essential that Christians re-emphasise the immense importance of the family unit and the creation ordinance of marriage. The foundation of the family unit consists of a stable, loving marriage relationship between a man and a woman in which children are conceived and brought up prayerfully, in the nurture of the Lord, then provided with security, love, understanding, and guidance. This is thoroughly biblical as we see, for example, in Deuteronomy 6:1-7, Ephesians 5:22-6:4 and Colossians 3:12-21.

Martin Luther, in his later social ethic, identified three offices or spheres, namely the family, government, and the church as expressing the rule of God in society. The foundational order is, however, the family, which Luther understood biblically as being like a school, which develops character and instruction in Scripture. Here, children learn to respect authority, people, and relationships, as well as how to make wise decisions and integrate gradually into society. In this context, the family unit includes the wider family of peers, grandparents, uncles, aunts, and cousins.

Megan was influenced considerably and mentored by her grandfather, referred to as Taid, a man who loved the Lord deeply and so naturally shared his faith with the family, and prayed for his family as well as others. Lindsay was influenced strongly by his grandmother, while Fiona was mentored by her godly parents. Steve refers to his mother being his mentor over the years but also his pastor in one period of his life. John-Mark suggests that parenting takes place in the early years and then, as children become older and more independent, some parenting continues but the relationship can move more into one of mentoring. The children can often begin to mentor the parents as well, but this depends on the kind of relationship established between parents and children. For David Koscol, an uncle was the one who assumed a mentoring role for him.

I was the first member in my family to become a Christian, followed by my younger brother a few months later, then our parents after about two years. I found it was far from easy sharing my Christian convictions and experience with my parents, largely due to my initial shyness and wondering how they might react. I prayed for them. When my brother was converted this was a huge help at home. I found it helpful also to introduce a few Christian friends from university to my parents; some were international students and keen Christians. One weekend I brought Daniel, from Sierra Leone, to stay at our home. He was a kind and warm believer, but imagine my shock before bedtime on the first evening when he asked about our family worship. Well, it did not exist, so he opened his Bible very naturally, read a few verses, and commented on them before praying. To my astonishment, my parents were impressed by his sincerity and warmth, which then gave us encouragement to follow his example tentatively. Certainly, meeting my Christian friends was instrumental in their coming to Christ in a preaching service a bit later. If your parents and peers are unbelievers, don't despair but pray for them, introduce them to Christians, invite them to services, but live consistently in the family! When my parents were converted, I found that I began, with my brother, to mentor them, which was a strange experience at first.

You may wonder how you fit into this picture if you are a young single person, recently married, or living at home with parents and peers. Here are a few general steps for you to consider, depending on your circumstances:

1. Marry only a believer of the opposite sex.

2. Is the believer you are attracted to a consistent Christian and eager to please the Lord? Is the person serious about a long-term relationship with you? Does the person really care for you or is it mostly a physical relationship?

3. Can you envisage spending a lifetime with that person? Do you share easily together personal concerns, interests, and a united desire to live for the Lord? Is the Lord and prayer at the centre of your relationship?

4. If you marry, begin well by praying and reading the Bible together daily. We describe this as family worship, and if children are born then they too should be brought into family worship at an early stage. Make sure you have time for one another with love, patience, kindness, self-sacrifice, and humility governing your relationship.

5. Ensure you settle in a local Bible-teaching church where you can find fellowship and support alongside opportunities for serving the Lord together.

6. If you observe a Christian or a couple in the church whom you respect and want to learn from, why not ask whether you can be mentored by them, or initially just meet them for fellowship at regular intervals and learn from them? This could lead on to a mentoring relationship.

7. If you have children, maintain biblical priorities and together be an example to your children, giving them time and much love as well as sharing your priorities with them. Enjoy the children too, and you may soon be mentoring them, or they will even be mentoring you!

8. If you are single, enjoy your family. Make more effort to get alongside them and learn from their own experience, whether they are Christians or not. Also, get to know other Christians and Christian families

in the church, and remember that God has a plan for your life.

Expectations

Lindsay hinted that the term 'mentoring' needs careful handling. And that is salutary advice.

Lindsay prefers to speak of mentoring as 'the deliberate investment in the spiritual development of other believers', exemplified in the life and ministry of the Lord Jesus, as in Luke chapters 8-10. That is key in understanding mentoring. Investment in encouraging and influencing others biblically, but naturally, is what is needed. Lindsay warns us about 'intense investment', for it can create problems along the line, like overdependence and a stifling of the mentee's personal development and decision-making. The mentor's aim must always be to disciple and encourage Christ-likeness, rather than to clone themselves. Remember, too, that all mentors are fallible, so never regard a mentor as always being right in what they say. Lindsay's experience of being mentored/ influenced by a number of people over the years, individuals who influenced him deeply and in different ways, is a healthy approach and avoids overdependence on one person, and possible abuse.

Fiona's threefold classification of mentoring is important, and so is the way that her personal mentor relationship 'just happened' naturally in the Lord's providence. She views mentoring as 'a walking alongside' in which both mentee and mentor 'click' and are able to be natural and relax with one another. Trust and confidentiality are obviously key aspects here, which need to be safeguarded. You may like to mull over John-Mark's classification of mentoring but also to 'rediscover the value and experience of true friendship and relationships', which is desperately needed in our 'broken' society.

Privileges: in Christ

However much mentoring is needed today in Churches, Christian Unions, and other areas of the Lord's work, we should not become obsessed with the idea. And there are good reasons for making that statement. Mentoring, despite its many advantages, is not the most important thing in a Christian's life. Allow me to explain.

First of all, Christians are privileged to be *'in Christ'*, spiritually and intimately related to the risen, glorified Christ. We were objectively chosen by the Father to be 'in Christ' from eternity (Eph. 1:3-6), but a miracle is required to make that objective union a reality in our lives. The Holy Spirit alone does this miracle (John 3:3-7) in regeneration or new birth, which is a radical, spiritual, and transforming work. Experientially, this brings us into intimate union and fellowship with Christ (John 15:1-8; Gal. 2:20). In trusting in Christ, you are also declared right and not guilty before the holy God, on the grounds of the sacrifice of the Lord Jesus Christ on the cross for your sin. That is what 'justify' or 'justified' means in the Bible. At Calvary, He dealt with our sin problem: its guilt, punishment and power. Now the same Holy Spirit remains within believers, guiding, strengthening, and keeping them in this intimate union with Christ.

As a Christian, therefore, your identity is in Christ. Is your personal identity a problem? Are you asking questions like: who am I? Is there a purpose in life? Do you long to be accepted and loved by someone? Well, God accepts you – but in Christ. You can never deserve His love and your privileges in Christ. He loves us as we are, whoever we are and whatever we have done. His love is vast and free; He can transform your life by His power and grace. He loves you, cares for you, guides and supports you all the way. This is a most precious relationship – Christ in you.

Secondly, enjoy and develop your personal relationship with the Lord Jesus Christ. Paul longed to know the Lord better, despite his years of being a Christian and a preacher (Phil. 3:10). He lived for Christ (Phil. 1:21), loving and serving Him deeply. Make this a priority in your life too (Matt. 6:33). One of my missionary friends, whom I knew well, was a midwife working in a remote part of the Middle East. Her call to overseas work was a result of someone asking her if she loved Jesus Christ. Her answer was positive. The question was repeated a second and third time, so her final answer was, 'I think so'. The questioner then illustrated his question: 'Does the Lord Jesus fill your life like my big feet fill my shoes?' The Lord used that conversation to convict her of compromise in lifestyle and half-hearted discipleship. After a few days she could say honestly before the Lord that she loved Him with all her heart. That is what God expects of *all* Christians, not just missionaries or Christian leaders/preachers (Deut. 6:4-5; Mark 12:29-34), and that includes mentors and mentees. It is our privilege to love the Lord, to please Him in obeying Him, spending time in His presence. Christians are in a love relationship with the Lord Jesus!

Mentoring involves loving Christ 100%

Yes, mentoring and being alongside another Christian can be extremely useful and enriching. I want to encourage mentoring in our Christian circles. I have benefited from being mentored, and I want many others to be encouraged and helped in this way.

However, I have a final word of advice. I felt the need for mentoring, especially in my early years as a Christian, and benefited enormously from godly individuals who at various stages influenced and mentored me. What attracted me to them? There was a freshness and vitality about their faith. They loved Christ so much. He was at the centre of their lives, their families, and their work. I was drawn to them like a magnet. Their lives were consistent. They loved and cared about people. Also, they prayed and enjoyed praying, even wanting me to pray with them on occasions when we met. Although very busy and in demand, they always had time for someone like myself. They came alongside me and encouraged me. I knew I could trust them. Anything personal I shared I knew they would regard as confidential and not share it with others. They were authentic and real about loving Christ, living for Christ, and encouraging others to do the same. They would phone me at times or send a letter to check how I was coping. I could ask them for advice and share a problem with them. When we met, apart from praying, their emphasis would be on pleasing Christ and depending on Him fully. It was so obvious to me that these men were in love with the Lord Jesus.

I emphasise this point because the quality of our relationship with the Lord will affect our relationships with others, even without us realising. In calling for mentoring – and it is an urgent call I am making in this book – this is the kind of mentor that is required. Let's be real with the Lord and be prepared to come alongside others in caring and praying for them. This is, first of all, a call to prayer, love, obedience, and then action – but all for the glory of the Lord Jesus Christ!

Questions:

1. *What is your reaction to the importance of family influence/ mentoring mentioned in some of the testimonies? Do you have stories to relate concerning spiritual influences within your family?*
2. *How are you seeking to be an influence within your family? Do you need help?*
3. *Are there expectations you have in terms of mentoring or being mentored?*

4. *'Rediscover the value and experience of true friendship and relationships' today. Is this important for you? What are you doing about it?*
5. *Can you explore and discuss your privileges and responsibilities as a Christian 'in Christ' with others?*
6. *What are the features that may attract you towards a mentor?*
7. *Do you find your personal identity in Christ? What could this mean to you in your personal life?*

Further Reading

I may surprise you in that I am not referring to books dealing directly with the subject of mentoring. This book is only an introduction to the subject of mentoring, and there are good resources available on the subject, which you can check out online.

For further reading I am being different, and for two major reasons.

Bible

*The first reason is that **the Bible is our main reference book on the subject**.* That is why I want you to read carefully, as a follow-up to this book, a few key passages in Scripture, already referred to in earlier chapters. You will find this rewarding.

a) Read carefully through the **four Gospels,** and observe the way our Lord Jesus mentored His disciples over a three-year period. Lindsay, for example, referred to Luke chapters 8-10.

b) Read the following passages in the Bible, noting important aspects of mentoring:
   - Acts 9:26-28; 11:22-26.
   - 1 Timothy
   - 2 Timothy
   - Titus, especially chapter 2:1-10.

Biography

The second reason for the unusual details of my Further Reading concerns two books, and I want to share them with you and urge you to read them. One book is by a former missionary to Africa, *Enough*, by Dr Helen Roseveare (Ross-shire: Christian Focus, 2011).

This is a small paperback worth its weight in gold. And it is an easy but challenging read. Helen shares briefly her struggles with singleness, and cruel experiences in Africa, including rape, a critical illness, then loneliness coupled with fear. There were struggles like rebelling at times against God's will, self-pity, and complaining. In her closing years, she suffered from Alzheimer's.

Enough describes how through these different experiences, however horrible and unwelcome, the Lord Jesus Christ was 'Enough' and sufficient for her. He was *'enough for happiness and contentment'* (emphasis added)in all her deep struggles.

This is a gem of a book. Please read it. You will be challenged concerning the all-sufficiency of Christ and the importance of your relationship with Him. Whether or not you have a mentor or are mentoring others, you need to see your identity and sufficiency in Christ. That will speak volumes to people too!

I confess that I authored the second book I am commending to you for further reading: *No Difficulties with God : The Life of Thomas Charles, Bala (1775-1814)*, (Ross-shire: Christian Focus, 2022).

Why do I commend this book? Well, I am eager to introduce you to an outstanding Christian, preacher, Church worker, missionary, and Bible scholar whose influence became international during, and even after, his lifetime. His story has had a profound impact on my personal relationship to the Lord, and my attitude towards mentoring.

And he himself mentored and cared for many Christians. Others also mentored him, even men like John Newton, who encouraged him and walked alongside him for some years. But I commend the book for another reason too. His love of the Lord was deep and the Gospel of Christ meant everything to him. He lived a life of unselfish devotion to Christ and His work. Christ, too, was very real and glorious to him.

You will see here some encouraging examples of mentoring and 'influencing' of young Christians.

Happy reading!

Christian Focus Publications

Our mission statement –

STAYING FAITHFUL
In dependence upon God we seek to impact the world
through literature faithful to His infallible Word, the
Bible. Our aim is to ensure that the Lord Jesus Christ is
presented as the only hope to obtain forgiveness of sin,
live a useful life and look forward to heaven with Him.

Our books are published in four imprints:

CHRISTIAN
FOCUS

Popular works including
biographies, commentaries, basic
doctrine and Christian living.

CHRISTIAN
HERITAGE

Books representing some of
the best material from the rich
heritage of the church.

MENTOR

Books written at a level
suitable for Bible College
and seminary students,
pastors, and other serious
readers. The imprint includes
commentaries, doctrinal
studies, examination of
current issues and church
history.

CF4•K

Children's books for quality Bible
teaching and for all age groups:
Sunday school curriculum, puzzle
and activity books; personal
and family devotional titles,
biographies and inspirational
stories – because you are never
too young to know Jesus!

Christian Focus Publications Ltd,
Geanies House, Fearn, Ross-shire,
IV20 1TW, Scotland, United Kingdom.
www.christianfocus.com